W9-AHT-252

Praise for
Marketing in the Moment, First Edition

"Michael's 3.0 marketing strategies took my business from a dying brick and mortar company to a profitable online money-making machine. I've reduced overhead and increased profit while spending more time with my family and less time in my business!"

—**Matthew Ferry**, bestselling author of *Creating Sales Velocity,* the "Players' Coach," www.matthewferry.com

"I highly recommend this book! It is a must-read for anyone wanting to learn from one of the top marketing minds in the world!"

—**Bill Bartmann**, self-made billionaire and two-time National Entrepreneur of the Year, Founder of Billionaire Business Systems

"Want to get ahead of your competition, fast? Then read *Marketing in the Moment.* Tasner's strategies focus on the future of online marketing, Web 3.0. This is innovative and forward-thinking material that is also practical and easy to use. Tasner has written the perfect desk reference for any online marketer!"

—**Joel Comm**, *New York Times* bestselling author of *Twitter Power*

"Forget asking your teenager or your computer geek how to navigate Web changes that keep coming at us faster and faster. They may know what button to push, but they know nothing about how to adapt marketing to keep up with these changes! *Marketing in the Moment* replaced my fear of the unknown in this rapidly changing online marketing environment and replaced it with security that I can actually know what I need in order to make the very best marketing decisions to boost my company profits. As a 25-year-old successful entrepreneur, Michael Tasner brings us his generation's unique know-how and ease of adaptability in the ever-shifting sands of new technology, and as a successful marketing expert he explains exactly what I need to do with my marketing to make it work in this environment."

—**Amy Levinson**, MPA, Executive Vice President, Guerrilla Marketing International, www.gmarketing.com

"If you want to make serious money online using the latest strategies, you've got to devour Michael Tasner's hot new book called *Marketing in the Moment*. I loved it!"

—**Robert G. Allen**, author of the bestsellers *Multiple Streams of Income*, *Multiple Streams of Internet Income*, *The One Minute Millionaire*, *Creating Wealth*, and *Cash in a Flash: Fast Money in Slow Times*

"*Marketing in the Moment* is an innovative guide to the future transition of online marketing. Tasner lays out the strategies and tools that are necessary to survive in this competitive market. This book is chock full of ideas that will help you maintain an edge on the competition."

—**Fran Capo**, five-time world record holder, motivational speaker, comedienne, author of *The Secrets of Publicity*

"Michael Tasner has written a powerful, down-to-earth guide and insightful book on one of the most important topics today—the next wave in online marketing. *Marketing in the Moment* will give you the tools you need to succeed in the next decade and beyond!"

—**M. Scott Carter**, Vice President, Sports 1 Marketing (Warren Moon Enterprises)

"*Marketing in the Moment* is full of new online marketing strategies that will inspire you to take action! Tasner delivers in-depth ideas and insights that *anyone* can utilize. Don't get passed by your competitors, step up and learn the new Web 3.0 tactics that will push you ahead of the pack!"

—**Greg Clement**, Business Guru, www.idontliketowork.com

"Anyone looking to become invaluable online should invest in this book. *Marketing in the Moment* provides immediately actionable steps anyone can use to connect with customers and establish themselves as irreplaceable."

—**Dave Crenshaw**, author of *Invaluable;* Founder, InvaluableInc.com

"After reading *Marketing in the Moment,* I wondered how my life may be different if I had this knowledge even a year ago. I would have saved time, money, and effort. The information is concise, timely, and effective."

—**Dr. John Spencer Ellis**, CEO, National Exercise & Sports Trainers Association; creator of the movie *The Compass*

"With the rapid change for marketers and businesses, knowing the right thing to do is a must! It's do or die. *Marketing in the Moment* gives the reader the right tools to win and now!"

—**Jeffrey Hayzlett**, author of *The Mirror Test*; Chief Marketing Officer, Kodak

"The online marketing world is changing fast and nobody knows for sure what's coming next. This book can help you be better prepared for the changes that are already afoot."

—**Tony Hsieh**, author of *Delivering Happiness;* CEO, Zappos

"As a publicity coach and publicity thought leader, I can safely say that this book is definitely an online marketing wake-up call! Web 2.0 is out, Web 3.0 is in! One of the many things I loved about this book is that Tasner provides you real-world examples of all the strategies he talks about. His in-depth descriptions are easy to follow and understand, so you can take them and implement them in your own business."

—**Dan Janal**, Founder, PR LEADS, www.prleadsplus.com

"Michael Tasner is a pioneer in sharing the inside secrets of the next generation of online marketing—also known as Web 3.0 marketing. If you read this book, you'll be ahead of the curve and get a lead on your competitors. If not, your marketing will become obsolete."

—**Manny Goldman**, CEO, Personal Growth Marketing; Founder, PersonalGrowth.com

"*Marketing in the Moment* oozes with opportunity. It's filled with powerful, profitable, and practical ideas on using Web 3.0 technology to take your business to the next level. Get started today."

—**Jill Konrath**, bestselling author of *SNAP Selling* and *Selling to Big Companies*

"Michael Tasner, with his on-target book, *Marketing in the Moment*, has gotten in front of the wave with present marketing trends. We are an 'I want it now' society. The book is easy to read and navigate, with numerous valuable resources. I love the Case Studies and Checklists, but the To Do lists are worth a million bucks! If you want to dominate your niche in today's market, you need this book!"

—**Robby LeBlanc**, www.MarketingYouCanUse.com

"Michael's book is right on target. What I love most about the book are the step-by-step instructions. Too many marketing books are filled with theory, and this one is all meat. If you want to sell more products or services online, you need this one right away!"

—**Ryan Lee**, entrepreneur, author, coach, www.ryanlee.com

"When I first met Michael Tasner, I instantly knew he was qualified to write this book. Why? Because of his unique business card that stood out from the crowd of about 40 others that I met that day. He practices what he preaches. This book is easy to read, well explained, and most of all, practical. Buy it, take action with the enclosed To Do's, and I know you'll profit."

—**Andrew Lock**, www.HelpMyBusiness.com, the #1 WebTV show for entrepreneurs

"Think you know it all about online marketing? Then read *Marketing in the Moment* and be blown away by the future of the Internet, Web 3.0! Michael Tasner is a leading marketing expert who delivers this ingenious guide to online marketing. I know that this book is full of strategies that will get you ahead of the competition and make you more money."

—**Eric Lofholm**, author of *How to Sell in the New Economy*

"I highly recommend this book! It is a must-read for anyone wanting to learn from one of top marketing minds in the world!"

—**Jill Lublin**, international speaker and bestselling author

"I am of the belief that *everything* is shifting. That the paradigm within which we've been operating, in business specifically, has gone bankrupt. That the way we've done things up until now—the way we've created, marketed, and distributed content; the way we've communicated with our partners, vendors, and customers; the mindset behind delivering our bottom line; and every other component in how we do business—has actually expired and a new model is emerging.

"As a huge believer that this twenty-first century shift in business is grounded and founded in collaboration and contribution, I was thrilled beyond measure to see that these are two concepts Tasner points to in *Marketing in the Moment*.

"I know that where we're going to start seeing this shift evidenced loudly is in the world of marketing. Tasner may be talking about Web 3.0, but what he's actually doing is *exemplifying* this twenty-first century shift in business.

"The content he provides is rich and exceedingly helpful in taking readers by the hand and crossing them over the bridge as we make this transition into the new paradigm for doing business. The most powerful piece for me, however, is in witnessing Tasner as an actual demonstration of what twenty-first century business is all about.

"I know *Marketing in the Moment* will prove to be a manual for those of us seeking support as we forge forward even further into this digital age."

—**Liora Mendeloff**, CEO and Founder, InstantMediaKit.com

"Michael Tasner has unlocked the vault to his multimillion dollar mind and given you *everything* you need to be successful on the Web today! Rarely does someone of Michael's stature reveal such profound secrets (the secrets he uses to run his own business!), and if that weren't enough, he also makes it so simple to follow his lead and execute his strategies. He's really taken the complexity out of it. If you want to succeed on the Web today, whether you want to do it yourself or you just want to disqualify 90% of the 'Web designers' out there who want to 'help' you, this is the book for you. This book is an absolute *must*-read."

—**Nick Nanton**, Esq., "The Celebrity Lawyer," www.DicksNanton.com

"*Marketing in the Moment* is a must-read for any marketer or business professional! Tasner divulges amazing strategies, tips, and ideas that will push you to the forefront of online marketing. Not only is the information critical to stay ahead of the competition, but he lays it out in a practical, easy-to-use format. This book is an amazing guide for anyone, from marketing novices to experienced veterans!"

—**Ed Oakley**, Founder and CEO, Enlightened Leadership Solutions, Inc.

"Folks, do buy this book and read it immediately. Web 2.0 is over-saturated and dying. Web 3.0 is where you should be. It's targeted and does not soak up your time. Tasner shows you exactly what it is and how you can take advantage of it. Super information and simply written."

—**Srikumar S. Rao**, author of *Happiness at Work: Be Resilient, Motivated and Successful—No Matter What*, TED speaker

"There is a ton of stuff written about Web 2.0 marketing but very little about Web 3.0 marketing. This book changes that completely. If you are looking to grab some low-hanging fruit, now is the time using Tasner's tactics!"

—**Freddie Rick**, Founder, BetterTrades

"When it comes to marketing on the Web, it's not just advisable to keep up with the trends, it's essential. Where and how people seek out information continues to change, and the key to successful marketing is to identify what's happening and adapt early on.

"If you don't reach your customers first, someone else will. "In this no-nonsense, easy-to-read guide, Michael Tasner breaks down today's top emerging marketplaces, devices, and technology to help your business stay one step ahead.

"You'll learn what to look for, how to take action, and most importantly, how to get results. You'll master Web 3.0 marketing before your competitors have Facebook figured out."

—**David Rivers**, President, KegWorks.com

"Put on your seat-belt[el]if propelling your personal brand or corporate brand is a goal or challenge on your dashboard. Michael Tasner's *Marketing in the Moment* is a must in the equation of Web 3.0 success."

—**Kenneth J. Skiba**, Sales Leader & CEO, YouHaveGotToBeKidding.com

"Web 2.0 is old news—Web 3.0 is in! Tasner unleashes his marketing expertise to educate you on the future of online marketing. *Marketing in the Moment* is an easy-to-use guide for any business professional, marketer, or sales person who wants to be ahead of the competition and make more money. If that sounds good to you, then you need to read this book."

—**Melanie Benson Strick**, CEO, Success Connections, Inc., www.successconnections.com

"Why go to an expensive Internet marketing course when everything you need for Web 3.0 is right here in Michael Tasner's excellent book *Marketing in the Moment*? With Internet marketing growing by leaps and bounds, it might seem difficult to keep up. But after reading Tasner's book, learning his many easy-to-learn practical strategies, I'm ready to conquer the Internet. I strongly recommend this book."

—**Joseph Sugarman**, Chairman, BluBlocker Corporation; author of *Advertising Secrets of the Written Word*

"Michael Tasner's new book will rock your world! He shares and teaches absolutely the most current, cutting edge strategies to successfully market your product or business on the Internet. If you are in business and you are online, you need this book."

—**Dan Thurmon**, author of *Off Balance On Purpose*

"This powerful book is loaded with great ideas to help you attract more customers and make more sales— immediately!"

—**Brian Tracy**, author of *The Art of Closing the Sale*

"'In the moment' means having a connection with your customers and marketing with authenticity. In this book, Tasner lays out a plan any business owner or sales professional can use to connect authentically in a way never before possible. Chapter 6 alone is worth the price of the entire book. Buy it or be left behind."

—**Jimmy Vee and Travis Miller**, bestselling authors of *Gravitational Marketing: The Science of Attracting Customers,* Founders of GravitationalMarketing.com

Marketing in the Moment
Second Edition

Marketing in the Moment

The Digital Marketing Guide to Generating More Sales and Reaching Your Customers First

Second Edition

Michael Tasner

© 2015 by Pearson Education, Inc.
Upper Saddle River, New Jersey 07458

For information about buying this title in bulk quantities, or for special sales opportunities (which may include electronic versions; custom cover designs; and content particular to your business, training goals, marketing focus, or branding interests), please contact our corporate sales department at corpsales@pearsoned.com or (800) 382-3419.

For government sales inquiries, please contact governmentsales@pearsoned.com.

For questions about sales outside the U.S., please contact international@pearsoned.com.

Company and product names mentioned herein are the trademarks or registered trademarks of their respective owners.

All rights reserved. No part of this book may be reproduced, in any form or by any means, without permission in writing from the publisher.

Printed in the United States of America

First Printing December 2014

ISBN-10: 0-13-388981-5
ISBN-13: 978-0-13-388981-9

Pearson Education LTD.
Pearson Education Australia PTY, Limited.
Pearson Education Singapore, Pte. Ltd.
Pearson Education Asia, Ltd.
Pearson Education Canada, Ltd.
Pearson Educación de Mexico, S.A. de C.V.
Pearson Education—Japan
Pearson Education Malaysia, Pte. Ltd.

Library of Congress Control Number: 2014952171

Editor-in-Chief
Amy Neidlinger

Executive Editor
Jeanne Glasser Levine

Operations Specialist
Jodi Kemper

Cover Designer
Chuti Prasertsith

Managing Editor
Kristy Hart

Project Editor
Andy Beaster

Copy Editor
Deadline Driven
Publishing

Proofreader
Deadline Driven
Publishing

Indexer
Deadline Driven
Publishing

Compositor
Deadline Driven
Publishing

Manufacturing Buyer
Dan Uhrig

To my beautiful daughter Emma Rose.

Table of Contents

Acknowledgments

I am thrilled with the success of the first book to be writing this second edition. My biggest thank you goes out to you, the readers. Thank you for purchasing the book, thank you for your case studies, your emails, your social media notes, and even your phone calls. What drives me is to see people putting the material into action and growing their businesses.

Of course, a special thank you to my editor Jeanne Levine and the entire team at Pearson. You all rock!

About the Author

Michael Tasner has been called by many as one of the top marketing experts in the world. He built a successful digital marketing and design agency from the ground up and had the honor to run digital marketing for some of the biggest speakers, authors, coaches, consultants, and entrepreneurs in the world. He has also consulted with numerous Fortune 1000 firms on their Web strategies.

Michael is the former Chief Marketing Officer for Guerrilla Marketing International, and he is hand trained by the father of Guerrilla Marketing, Jay Conrad Levinson. Michael currently runs the premier marketing training company on the planet, No Joke Marketing®.

Michael lives in Niagara Falls, NY with his wife Anna, twin boys Connor and Logan, and daughter Emma.

Introduction

There has never been a better time in history than now to be deploying digital marketing for your business. It's the fastest growing set of marketing strategies on the planet and the one that will continue to define how well your business does.

The first edition of *Marketing in the Moment* came out in 2010. I'm very proud to say that the core of the book was spot on. If anything, some of the strategies were a bit ahead of their time. For example, mobile marketing was the cornerstone of the book. Now, several years later, everywhere you turn, marketing gurus are touting that it's the hottest trend on the planet. Why do I share that with you? To let you know you've made the right choice in purchasing and reading this book. There are trends and tactics in here that will put you years ahead of your competition, allowing you to snatch up market share before your competitors even know what hit them.

This newly revised edition contains all of the latest and greatest digital marketing strategies that have evolved over the past few years and trends that are coming down the pipeline. The most important objective I have for you in this second edition is to ensure you are armed and up to date with everything you need to dominate the marketplace.

With the goal of market domination at the forefront of your mind, you also must be aware of a few of the challenges that could stop you in your tracks. The biggest challenge today is the continually growing amount of competition in the marketplace. Let's say you run a flower shop. A few years ago, you may have had a handful of local competitors. Not only has the number of local retail-based competitors most likely risen, but you are also now faced with the dozens of online competitors who have large budgets that you most likely can't come close to matching. Armed with the materials in this book, I will show you how to compete head on and grow your business faster using digital marketing.

If you look around you or listen to the news, you have heard and will continue to hear about retail businesses going under. Although this isn't a book on business success, when I've analyzed this trend of failing businesses, it largely comes down to those businesses not staying up to date with all of the digital marketing trends. Wouldn't it be easier to stay in business if your digital marketing efforts were driving more people to your retail outlet? I'd think so.

The other challenge to keep in mind is that both consumers and businesses have shifted the way they purchase products and services, and even more important is that they have shifted the way they research and find these products and services. This is where we as marketers need to focus our attention. We need to be certain that we are marketing in the right places and at the right time while grabbing the attention of consumers and businesses. This is why e-commerce companies have recently fared much better than direct retail competition. They have adopted the changes and are aware of the shifts, and they are doing everything they can to grab new customers and keep their current customers buying more.

How would you like to be ahead of 98 percent of other marketers, gain an unfair advantage over your competitors, and start grabbing market share before anyone realizes they should have been doing the same for the past year?

Hopefully, you answered yes. I mean, who wouldn't want to be on the leading edge and grabbing market share before all the rest do? Before telling you how this is going to happen, let's take a step back and put some things into perspective.

Recognize Any of These?

Sit back for a second and think about this first set of terms:

> collaboration, blogging, content sharing, online video, social media

Now think about this second set of terms:

> mobile browsing, MMS marketing, live streaming video, social advertising, microblogging, extreme personalization, retargeting, augmented reality

Chances are, you recognize many more terms in the first group than in the second. There is some good news, but also some bad news. The good news is that if you are familiar with the first set of terms and are deploying some of the tactics, you are moving in the right direction. The not-so-great news is that the second set of words must also be added to your marketing dialogue, and fast, as this is where the marketing landscape is continuing to head.

What Does This Mean to You?

In uncertain economic times, we cannot ignore trends. If I'm saying that mobile marketing is the hottest trend since sliced bread and you need to jump on it, I mean it. The new digital marketing techniques cannot be ignored, unless you are looking for your competitors to grab your market share and drive you out of business. The key is to get traction for multiple digital marketing sources. If one dries up, no worries because you have another 15 that feed the business. Embrace the changes and watch your business thrive.

Move Out of the Way, or Jump on the Bullet Train

Marketing in the Moment is meant to serve as your step-by-step guidebook to allow you to profit from the latest and greatest digital marketing techniques. If you're not ready to be on the forefront of the marketing world, this book is not for you.

Why Should You Listen to Me?

I'm an avid reader myself. I've read thousands of books and taken hundreds of courses. The content that resonated the best with me is content that came from authors being in the field and in the trenches. I only wanted to know what worked and what didn't work, backed with case studies. That is the approach I take with this book.

From a "resume" standpoint, here are the details that show you I've been in the fields and am constantly in the fields looking for what's next. I provide these details not to brag, but rather for you to know you are getting materials from a top marketing authority.

I used to run a nice-sized online marketing and design firm. I started the company when I was quite young and grew it deploying the tactics I teach in this book. This company worked with some of the most high-profile speakers, authors, consultants, and entrepreneurs in the world. These businesses would hire my firm to essentially run their entire online marketing campaigns from A to Z. I've also consulted with numerous Fortune 1000 companies, teaching them how to implement the latest and greatest Web efforts in their marketing.

Among my favorite partnerships was the relationship I struck with Guerrilla Marketing International (the company started by Jay Conrad Levinson). I had the honor of assisting this company with its digital marketing, and ultimately, I became their Chief Marketing Officer for a few years.

Finally, I've had other businesses (six) where I've used these tactics to grow and dominate the marketplace. I'm here to teach you step by step to achieve the results you've been dreaming about.

How to Use This Book

I want this to be your desk reference to all things digital marketing. Read the book from cover to cover at least twice. This was written as a tactical book for a reason. One of the biggest complaints I would hear from people while in the field is the content they got from others was good, but they were still unsure how to implement the material. Take the famous movie *The Secret*. The movie was life-changing, but nowhere did it tell you how to actually start seeing some of the changes come into your day-to-day life. What I'm getting at here is this: There are no excuses as to why you can't implement this stuff. It's not too hard, and it's been boiled down for you. Take the steps and work them into your digital marketing today!

Throughout the book, you will see different symbols. Here are their meanings:

Checklist

You will find a variety of checklists and lists in general. These are there for your reference.

To Do

This book is light on fluff and heavy on tactics that will get you results. We will be talking about how to leverage certain marketing tactics. Under the To Do icon, you will see a pared-down list of action items for you to start implementing in ten steps or fewer.

Case Study

For each of the major marketing tactics we are teaching you about, a case study of how that tactic has been used in real life is included. Also included with the case study is the key result achieved from the tactic and the takeaway I want you to get.

Tas Tip

Tas Tips are the "ah-ha" points throughout the book.

FAQs

Before we get started, let's tackle some of the most frequently asked questions.

Do All the Tactics Apply to My Business?

The simple answer: yes. The tactics presented in this book are tactics that any business regardless of the shape and size can deploy immediately. With that said, I would be kidding myself if I assumed that you could put every technique into practice immediately. Look for the tactics that most apply to your business and put them into action. Once you have been successful with those, add more. Marketing is all about testing, tweaking, and improving.

Is Digital Marketing Expensive to Do?

Most of the tactics discussed are very low-cost but high-impact. Effective marketing does not necessarily mean that it needs to be costly. It does, however, need to produce results and have the ability to be tracked and then tweaked.

Who Does This Book Apply To?

Entrepreneurs, speakers, authors, consultants, home-based businesses, corporations looking to gain an edge, infopreneurs, and intrapreneurs can all benefit from this book.

Are There Other Tools in This Book Besides Online Marketing?

There are a ton of resources in this book for both offline and online use. Throughout the book, there is also a variety of practical, no-nonsense, business advice on general marketing. Plain and simple, I want your business to succeed. Leveraging innovative marketing tactics to increase your traffic and leads is simply one route to get you there quickly.

1

The Mindset Shift: From Web 2.0 Digital Marketing to Web 3.0 Digital Marketing and Beyond

What Is Web 2.0?

One of the big online buzz phrases that made its way around the world is Web 2.0.

Web 2.0 began when Web users started to drastically change the way they were using the Web on a day-to-day basis. The main trends that shaped Web 2.0 include content sharing, creativity, segmentation, social components, and a large move from static web sites and tools to more dynamic ones. Some of the added functionality is peer-to-peer sharing of files, easier communication and networking on various social marketing sites, video sharing, and blogging. Web directories evolved to social tagging, personal web sites shifted to blogs, and online versions of encyclopedias morphed into Wikipedia. In the Web 2.0 world, collaborating on social networks and sharing information helped shape the trend relatively quickly.

As a marketing advantage, there are four key components to Web 2.0:

- Social networks are the sites where people come together and share ideas, thoughts, and comments. Examples: Facebook, LinkedIn, and MySpace.

- Social media are the places where you can share content with the world in hopes of spreading awareness. Examples: YouTube, Scribd, Flickr, Instagram, and Pinterest.

- User-generated content was what sparked much of the discussion on Web 2.0. This is where users create, manage, and update information. Examples: Squidoo, blogs, Tumblr, and Wikipedia.

- Social news and bookmarking have allowed users to organize their Web experiences. Examples: Digg, Delicious, Technorati, and StumbleUpon.

The Limitations of Web 2.0 Thinking

Many people believe that Web 2.0 is where things stopped and that the Internet has simply evolved a bit more. I'm going to show you why this thinking is massively flawed and how you can capitalize on the newest trends. Remember, the intention is to make sure you are using the various tactics, but also paving the way to grab market share before your competitors do in the more up-to-date techniques.

Here are five factors that limit Web 2.0:

- Oversaturation
- Misconceptions
- Time

- Modes of Interaction
- Openness

Oversaturation

Let's start with the limiting factor that should command the most attention: oversaturation. The problem is that everyone and their third cousin are on the Web 2.0 bandwagon. Although they may fully understand their thinking is "Web 2.0" related, their actions prove otherwise.

As a society, we have become so obsessed with Web 2.0 that it has become oversaturated! All of this saturation causes an exorbitant amount of unnecessary noise. As someone who is trying to make sure your message is getting through, noise doesn't always work in your favor.

The key limitation to Web 2.0 is that it has become oversaturated. Here are some examples:

- Your grandma calls you and says she's been told she needs a blog so that her friends can stay updated on her travels.
- Eight-year-olds are posting videos on YouTube.
- Photos of your kid's birthday are shared with the world on Facebook and Instagram in close to real time.

You might argue that, as a result, these sites are receiving a lot of good traffic because everyone is logging on. You are correct. However, how targeted is the traffic going to be? This is a key concept you will hear throughout the book. Targeted traffic, or traffic that is ready, willing, and able to take in your message in the way that they want, is the advantage that strategic marketers seek.

When it comes down to it, the key is drilling down to find the best interaction. Facebook is an excellent place to network, meet new people, and do business. But Facebook is a powerful marketing tool only when you know how to use it to reach out to specific people or groups of people, even more so when you understand how to market to prospects who don't even realize you are doing so.

Misconceptions

Common misconceptions about Web 2.0 have also caused difficulties. From an overarching standpoint, the area that I have taken issue with is people saying that Web 2.0 has simply evolved to where it is at today. As you will soon learn, we are way past Web 2.0 marketing and into a new realm of marketing.

Time

Time is also a limiting factor. As we become more and more connected, we get more and more distracted by all the noise, such as comments being made on our blogs, questions about our photos on Instagram, or updates on Facebook. One trend that never seems to change is that people continue to get busier and have less time for interaction.

Both consumers and businesses continue to demand more information, and they want it faster, making it challenging to keep up. Once they think they have found their preferred method of communication (email), a better method comes out that is even faster (to be talked about shortly).

Modes of Interaction

I understand that this way of thinking may be contradictory to what you might be thinking: Isn't the goal of Web 2.0 to create new modes of interaction? I define modes of interaction as the different places and devices that people use to gather, search, network, and exchange information. People are gathering in different places around the Web and interacting in different ways with each other. But these modes of interaction have decreased the human touch. Do you even pick up a phone on a daily basis? If you need something, you pop off an email. If you have a question, you search Google and often land on Wikipedia.

Once you start getting bogged down with emails, Facebook messages, and status updates, you start to look for a solution to simplify things, and a bad taste forms in your mouth. Then you reach the tipping point, making you jump ship and focus on something else. In other words, there is just too much out there, thus causing confusion and a lack of adoption.

Openness

Lastly, the openness of Web 2.0 has become a striking limitation. Most humans are naturally private. When you have a Facebook account, a LinkedIn account, and an Instagram page, your privacy drops quickly. If you are an avid user of Facebook or read the news, you will remember when Facebook changed its policy to state that it owns your content even after you've canceled your account. The company did change that policy back, but it's still quite vague in its favor. We enjoy sharing details about ourselves, but there comes a point where it just gets weird or creepy.

So Where Are We at from a Digital Marketing Standpoint Today?

In the first edition of the book, I said we have shifted from Web 2.0 marketing to Web 3.0 marketing, coining the phrase Web 3.0 marketing. I believe that buzz phrase still holds true today. There isn't a better phrase to sum things up. Many marketers have called this the mobile era, for example. Although that is true, it doesn't encapsulate the entire *movement*. The sooner you start to realize how things have shifted so rapidly over the past year or so and how they are continuing to shift at a pace that is hard to keep up with, the quicker you will get to dominating in this movement.

So what does this new movement look like from a digital marketing standpoint? Simply, it is digital marketing spawned from the convergence of new technologies combined with rapidly changing consumer-buying trends and habits. An example is a prospect signing up for your text alerts he found on an infographic you posted on Pinterest. That alert then drives him to your mobile responsive web site where he makes a purchase while sitting at the park on his lunch break. To put things into perspective, here are the key overarching trends to this new marketing movement:

- **Social media on steroids.** Social media is everywhere we look. It is now fully integrated into our lives and often drives the way we make purchasing decisions. A few years ago, it was okay to grab an account on Facebook. Now you must have accounts on all the major social networks and content that is noteworthy if you expect to stand out in the crowd.

- **Unique experiences.** Experiences create memories that people talk about. From a digital standpoint, I'm a huge fan of live streaming video and even virtual reality worlds. Both of these settings are web-based, but they create unique experiences. People browse for products on sites like SecondLife.com and they watch live video events on LiveStream.com, all from the comfort of their homes.

- **Customization/personalization/targeted messages.** Who is at the center of the universe? You! We care about ourselves and our agenda. Some of the digital trends that have helped morphed this trend are things like augmented reality, retargeting, and more advanced segmentation software. These tools allow you to send the right message at the right time on the right platform.

- **In-the-moment decisions.** I have seen consumers make decisions much faster than a few years ago. This tends to apply to decisions that are not massive in nature (buying a new house, for example). The social-on-steroids trend has helped drive this one a bit, as you can get instant feedback on the decision you are about to make but also the ease of finding information on the Web. There are reviews everywhere and gobs and gobs of data. I've always stressed that you need to take swift action if someone is getting ready to do business with you. This action means making sure your reputation is solid online, but more so, using retargeting techniques to bring them back into your world.

- **Mobile everything.** The fastest-growing trend on the planet is mobile. Text messages have replaced the need to make phone calls, and iPhones are replacing the need to carry credit cards or cash. Sit just about any-where in public and you will find that the majority of those around you are on their phones. As a marketer, if we don't adapt to and capitalize on mobile, we are dead in the water.

- **Content craze.** There is a thirst for good content. As a consumer, the challenge is separating out the noise to quickly determine what "good" content is. This content craze has led to what many marketers call "inbound marketing." With inbound marketing, your prospects find the content you posted and come to you versus the other way around. This is a beautiful thing and can instantly add profits to your bottom line when deployed correctly. From a marketing standpoint, we are going to make sure we publish great content on a regular basis in the mediums our prospects want.

2

How Does Your Digital Marketing Look Today?

Times Are a Changing

We're getting ready to dive into the meat of the book, the action-taking stuff. Before we do, I want to throw a few final examples that will help hit things home if you are not convinced that times have changed quite a bit over the past few years.

Increasing Mobility and Reliance on Mobile Devices

Do you break into a sweat when you don't have your mobile device within arm's reach? Rarely does anyone go anywhere now without a mobile device. When you are shopping you may be talking to a friend, listening to a podcast, or more likely checking to make sure you are getting the best price possible on your potential purchases. The reliance on mobile devices is going to continue and is getting ready to get its second wind, helping propel it even further.

Social Shoppers

When was the last time you posted something on Facebook that started with, "I'm thinking of buying XYZ, what do you think?" or maybe something like, "Does anyone know a great place to do XYZ?" Most of us to go to our circle of friends or our network to get advice—whether that advice is to talk ourselves out of what we may do or to help reconfirm a purchasing decision. Combine this social shopping with browsing the company's Facebook page you are considering doing business with. If there are a bunch of negative comments on the page, that more than likely will sway you to change your mind. We are a social culture.

A Reduction in the Need to Be "Belly-to-Belly"

There are many reasons people are continuing to flock to the Web for virtual communication instead of jumping on a plane for a face-to-face meeting, with the largest reason being cost. It is expensive to fly across the country, stay in a hotel, dine out, take taxies, and on top of it all, miss both work and family time. Virtual trade shows are gaining in popularity. www.SecondLife.com continues to get larger, and services like www.GoToMeeting.com and www.WebEx.com are attracting new customers like crazy.

Once you go virtual, you may never want to fly again, at least for a business meeting. Once you go cam-to-cam, face-to-face will never be the same!

Everything Is Continuing to Go to the Web

Anything and everything continues to go to the Web. Twelve-year-olds are running million-dollar social networks; small pizza companies are taking orders through the Web;

your family diner has a few different apps and actively manages its comments on Facebook, Yelp, and Foursquare; your grandma is tweeting; and your long-lost cousin boasts 50,000 Pinterest followers. And the list goes on, and on, and on. This trend will not change.

Conducting a 360-Degree Review of Your Web Platform and Marketing Efforts

I'm a huge fan of 360-degree reviews. You may have heard of these. They are typically used in the Human Resource department of a company for employee reviews. The objective of the review is to get a view from all different angles (thus, the name 360 degrees) of the particular employee.

Here's how it works: You're an employee working at one of the large automakers (who will remain nameless). Assuming you still have a job, you work daily with other employees just like you, for a direct supervisor. And you have people reporting directly to you. In the process of conducting your review to decide whether you will get a two-cent-per-hour raise (I know, don't get too excited), your performance will be reviewed by your boss, your peers, and your own direct reports. This ensures that you're getting the most accurate representation of the quality of your work. It also serves as a great checks-and-balances system. If your boss didn't like you, that is only one leg of the review. And one of these days, you will be part of your boss's 360-degree review.

Now take that same thinking and apply it your marketing. When you complete this exercise, you will be able to spot things you may not have noticed before and laser in on the areas that pose the largest upside potential.

To Do

How to Conduct a 360-Degree Review of Your Web Efforts

Step 1.   Make a list of all the people who have a hand in or are touched by your marketing efforts.

For example: The CEO, your marketing director, marketing executives, salespeople, engineers, research and development folks, vendors, partners, and your customers. The key here is to make sure you are not leaving anyone out. If you miss one person, you are not fully getting a 360-degree review. You might get only 300 degrees.

Step 2.   Construct two to three surveys for those people to complete.

The first survey will go to all internal employees, the second to your vendors/partners, if applicable, and the last to your customers. It's up to you if you want to send this to all your customers. It depends highly on how many customers you have. If you're a smaller company, I recommend sending it to all your customers. If you're a larger company with thousands of customers, send it to enough clients to get a good response back. Typical response rates range from 3% to 10%. I've seen lower, but I've also seen response rates as high as 90%. But those are just the averages.

A few important notes on these surveys:

- I encourage you to send these 100 percent electronically. When sending surveys electronically, you have a much higher chance of getting a response. Various survey tools can be used, such as www.Survey Monkey.com, www.Zoomerang.com, www.keysurvey. com, and even Google Forms.

- Keep your surveys short to increase your response rate.

- Give some type of incentive for your outside vendors, partners, or customers to fill these out, and watch your response rates skyrocket. (For example, give them 10 percent off their next order.)

- Modify anything to fit your business.

I like allowing for comments after each question to solicit additional feedback. The reason I ask and solicit more open-ended feedback is to ensure that we don't miss any of the trends. If your customers are finding you in the underwater basket-weaving forum, and we don't leave open space for them to fill in that information, we will never discover that valuable information.

To get these forms in an editable format, visit www. marketinginthemomentbook.com/360.

Step 3. Compile the data.

This is going to take you quite a bit of time. Here are some tips for compiling the data:

- Many of the survey software tools will do this for you.

- Develop three different Microsoft Excel files and label them appropriately (internal, vendors/partners, and customers).

- Start with the quantifiable data and get that into Excel. Most likely, this will be a simple export.

- Move on to the open-ended questions. Take all the responses for each question and place them into Excel so you can see all the data in front of you.

- Scroll down the column of open-ended questions and look for trends. I like to use the find feature in Excel to see whether similar words are being found. For example, you can search for craigslist to see all the places it was mentioned.

- When you find similar answers in the open-ended questions, group those together.

- When you have this task done, you should be able to easily see the results for the quantifiable section, and all the answers to the open-ended sections grouped together with similar thoughts.

- Lastly, do the same thing with the comments as you did with the open-ended questions: Group similar comments together, using the find feature to aid in this task.

Step 4.   Interpret the data.

You now have your data organized in a much more logical format so that you can start figuring out what it all means. Print out all the sheets and spread them out across a long desk so you can see everything. What you're looking for here are trends across the various groups and weaknesses in your marketing strategy. Keep in mind that in this exercise, bad news is actually good—it's what you're looking for. It's great to see the good stuff, but we're more concerned with the areas in which you need to improve because these are your greatest opportunities for growth. What you are most likely going to find is two-fold:

First, 20 percent of your marketing is producing the most results. The other 80 percent is a waste of time, money, and energy.

Second, there are many new trends and places you can start leveraging in your online marketing strategy.

Step 5.   Compile your action plan, and continue reading this book!

When you were going through all the data, I guarantee that your results came back positive, but there are several places you can start capitalizing on your added insights.

The whole point of doing the 360-degree review is to give you a starting point that applies to your business. Every business is different. Not every marketing method is going to be right for your business, but some of them will. Armed with internal and external data, you can make the best decisions about how to move forward in your digital marketing.

Case Study

My video studio Guerrilla Video Solutions was looking for ways to generate new business. We turned to the 360-degree survey format. We interviewed our employees, contractors, vendors, and a variety of our customers to solicit targeted feedback. Because we were offering a $2,000 video package, the survey was upwards of 90 percent. Plain and simple, we got some solid feedback that allowed us to make the most informed and strategic decisions.

We were initially spreading our marketing a bit wider than I would have liked. We were doing various ad campaigns, were on all the major social media channels, doing some search engine marketing, and trying to further help word-of-mouth marketing.

After finishing the audit, we realized a variety of things:

- Google AdWords were a waste of money, because the phrases our customers were using were much more targeted and specialized. We assumed everyone simply typed in "video production," but they were typing in things like "video production for big event."

- Our prospects needed more case studies and education about the process. Good video isn't cheap, but it's a lot more affordable than our prospects and customers had thought. Most of our customers also had no idea about the various uses of video besides just placing it on their web sites and for television purposes.

- They hang out in a few key networking groups and a few strategic locally based social networks.

The result: We shifted our search engine optimization efforts and have already seen five times more targeted leads. We also added a variety of videos in the beginning of the sales cycle, which has led to a two times more conversion.

Investing in New and Additional Technologies

The good thing about digital marketing is that there are not a lot of expensive devices or systems I'd recommend you purchase. The key with technology (in my opinion) is that you always want to steer yourself to Web-based solutions. Even the software itself is available as Web-based applications. Don't go purchasing any chunky devices that seem to be the new best thing, because chances are the same system is available 100 percent Web-based at one-tenth of the cost.

To get ready, you'll need a basic tool kit of some technology and talent. Here are the fundamentals that we recommend you start adopting and implementing in your organization:

- A mobile marketing system. Visit www.marketinginthe-momentbook.com/mobile for my favorite tools.

- A Web-based customer relationship management system. My favorite is Salesforce.com.

- If you are going to process any orders online, you need a shopping cart tool and affiliate module. Visit www.marketinginthemomentbook.com/carts to get a list of a variety of the top carts.

- A mobile responsive web site. We will talk more about this, but this investment (depending on the size of your business and web site) could add up. However, out of all of the tools I've mentioned, this one would be the first one I tackled. If your web site does not look good on mobile devices, you are losing business daily.

- A few additional Web-based tools that will be discussed in detail in the book (like analytics, heat mapping, and retargeting).

- A platform to virtually communicate and collaborate across a company. My favorite tool for collaboration is

Google apps. This allows me to run companies without a physical office.

Check out these Google apps:

- Gmail
- Google Docs / Drive
- Google Forms
- Google Chat / Hangouts
- Google Calendars

We'll get back to discussing collaboration in Chapter 11, "Collaboration and Speed: The Secret Sauce to Marketing in the Moment."

For a list of all of the tools I recommend, visit www.marketinginthemomentbook.com/tools.

The Top Five Things You Need to Do to Master and Prepare for the Web 3.0 Wave

To recap, here's what you need to do:

- Recognize that times are changing and trends are shifting.
- Conduct a 360-degree online-marketing review to solicit feedback.
- Take the feedback to heart, and start implementing the changes.
- Invest in some new technology.
- Capitalize on and grab market share while everyone else is still in denial.

3

Social on Steroids: How to Correctly Capitalize on Social Media

About ten years ago (or so), you would often hear the phrase, "I don't think I really need a web site." This was a common phrase because business owners couldn't see where the future was headed. I'm not making them wrong for making that decision, but the ones who jumped on the bandwagon earlier on (early adopters) got to reap the bulk of the rewards.

If we fast forward, I am still hearing from many business owners that they don't feel the need for social media or see the value of social media. They understand the importance of having a web site, but most still can't see the value of Facebook, Pinterest, Instagram, Twitter, Vine, and beyond.

Did you know...
...Social media is the number one daily activity Americans spend time on? The time people spend engaged in the social media world beats out Google and email.

Though I hear the question "Do I really need social media?," it is the most talked about digital marketing buzz phrase out there. The social trend continues to widen as new social networks continue to hit the market and as users continue to desire more communication and to be highly mobile.

The challenge with all of the content and training on social media is that things have gotten complicated. There are 250-page books on each of the social media platforms and even magazines have been dedicated to some of the social networks. Although this is great, I want to give you social media in a much simpler fashion, and the tactics that "just work" in one chapter. I would rather see you take simple, profitable actions versus attempt to do 20 different things across each social network.

One additional point to keep in mind is that by the time of publication, there will most likely be a new hit social media platform that has several million users. That is what keeps things exciting in the social media world.

The Secret Sauce to Social Media

Social media marketing is the tactic of getting your content to a lot of eyeballs across social networking platforms. That content can be in the form of text, a video, a picture, a link, an infographic, and more. When you combine getting content out with connecting with people you start to move down the path of successful social media marketing.

Many business owners and marketers think there is a "secret sauce" when it comes to social media, a "covert" tactic to magically get 10,000 likes or hundreds of leads overnight. Unfortunately, there is no magic pill to social media (unless you are willing to shell out a lot of money in ad dollars on social media). Another issue is that most people have become obsessed with numbers, assuming that bigger is better and constantly striving to add more to their social networks. Though more numbers are great, you should be focused on relationships.

Although there is no magic pill for rapid social media growth, there are guiding principles you need to keep at the forefront of your social marketing efforts. I refer to these as the 10 social media commandments.

The 10 Commandments of Social Media

1. Reframe your brain. Instead of trying to get "bigger numbers," develop more authentic relationships and connections. Think of the Zappos style of customer service. The company encourages its customer service people to stay on the phone for as long as they need. It is easy to go out and get 5,000 Twitter followers, but they will be from 20 different countries and most likely spam accounts. It is better for you to have 100 Twitter followers who care about what you have to say and engage with you on a regular basis.

2. Social media marketing should be lumped in with your overall content marketing strategy. This is simply another method for getting your content out to people and connecting with them. Blogging goes hand in hand with social media as does search engine optimization.

3. Your overall marketing will get better with repetition. What I mean by this is simple: You generate better results if the same marketing message is being stated across social media along with email, direct mail, messages in your store, and so on. You shouldn't promote one thing on social media and then something totally different in your store front. If you do, you will confuse people. Repetition is your friend. Your prospects need to hear your message ten times or more to move into a buying readiness state so make sure you are firing on all cylinders and hitting them up from different channels and avenues.

4. Treat each social network differently. Every platform has its do's and do not's along with its quirks. What may work on Facebook may go over like a lead balloon on LinkedIn. Instead of just lumping all of your social marketing activities into one bucket, separate out each of the buckets and prepare unique original content for each.

5. Your prospects and customers expect fast responses, often within minutes or hours. If someone sends in a message or makes a comment reply as fast as you can, especially if it is an issue with your product or service. As time goes on, people get angrier and angrier. We are trying to prevent social media disasters. I would worry if you have an angry customer who is logged into a social media platform.

6. Frequency matters. If you have enough to say several times during the day, post several times a day. If the content is mere filler content, leave it out. You need to make sure your social media presence doesn't get stale. One of my reliable methods for posting if I am focused on a local market is to talk about a new restaurant or an upcoming event or festival in the area.

7. At the end of the day, the purpose of marketing is to drive profits. When posting good content, you should generate more interest, but often your prospects need to be moved along a bit. Do not be afraid to go in for the close or go in for the ask once or twice a week. I like to balance three to four non-sales pieces of content with 1 sales piece of content.

8. Social media is about engagement. I tend to get better results when I engage with someone on social media. For example, on Twitter.com, I like to seek out people mentioning a particular phrase and I write them a message comment on their tweet. This generates engagement and new followers.

9. I understand that most people are impatient, and they want better and faster results. Marketing takes time, there is no question about it. However, there is a way to generate some faster traction with social media. The

simple answer is through ad spend. Most of the big social networking sites are now generating the bulk of their revenue by allowing people to advertise on their site. If you are looking for quick targeted Facebook followers (as an example), Facebook ads are your answer.

10. From a content perspective, the best content that will get viewed the most and shared the most is content that is authentically helpful. When I say the word authentic, I mean content that hasn't been modified or morphed to serve your business of generating more business. Here is an example to further drive this point home. Let's say that you sell gunite pools and you want to educate people and provide authentically helpful content on selecting the right type of pool. If you had a hidden agenda in mind, you would make sure that the content you put out was slanted to show that gunite pools are superior to any other type of pool (fiberglass and liner pools, for example) because you want more sales. Unfortunately, this content is not authentically helpful as you will be doing some people a disservice that really shouldn't get a gunite pool because a vinyl pool will be better for their needs. To provide authentically helpful content, put together an unbiased infographic showing the pros and cons to each of the different types of pools. While some people may end up putting in a different type of pool using a different vendor, they will remember that you helped them. They will refer friends, provide positive reviews online, and share the content for you. That is how you earn business and dominate from a content perspective.

The Big Six

At the time of writing this book, there are tens of thousands of social networking platforms. I have zoned in on the top six social networking channels that I recommend focusing on at this time.

I promised some media condensed. Each social network presented in the following sections has three points of content: Why should you use the network, who should look at using it, and how do you get traction with the network and get rolling? Ready? Let's go.

YouTube

Why?

YouTube is the world's second largest search engine and a powerhouse of a web site. What makes this a great platform for marketing is simple: People prefer to watch a video versus any other marketing medium. Video produces better conversions, more conversations, and simply better results. With the rise of mobile, everyone is now a publisher and can produce content quickly and easily.

Who?

This is a platform that makes sense for any type of business owner. There is not one business that I can think of that wouldn't benefit from being on YouTube.

How?

1. Create your YouTube channel.

2. Optimize the channel with a good keyword rich description and some good graphics to match.

3. Start producing short educational videos (1–3 minutes in length), and load up one or two videos a day for a month.

4. Make sure each video is optimized for search (video title, keywords, description, and tags).

5. Keep your video channel fresh with new and engaging content on a regular basis.

6. Comment on others videos, and mention the link in your video. Please don't spam, but comment on videos

when it would make sense for people to watch your videos as well.

Google+

Why?

Anything that Google owns, I like to be a part of (Google also owns YouTube.com). Google+ is a network that is focused on providing relevant content to people. There are a lot of interesting and useful features that can keep your targeting focused. There are also a lot of tie ins to Google+ and ranking higher in the search engines.

Who?

This platform is not one I recommend jumping on unless you already crank on sites like Facebook and YouTube. If you have a lot of content that can keep your Google+ page stocked, this is a great platform, but not one that you can get away with posting on only once every few weeks.

How?

1. Although business pages can do well, I have seen much better results when focusing on a personal Google+ profile. By way of personal, I mean one that is centered around a person or name versus a business name. Build out your profile, optimize it for search, and start to get some people in your circles.

2. Leverage circles to the fullest. Circles are among my favorite feature of Google+. You put people into different circles and have certain content shown to only those people. Think of where this could come in handy. One example is prospects for customers. You don't want to annoy your customers with offers to buy your service if they have already done so. Set up a few different circles and customize the content for those customers.

3. Contribute to the various Google+ communities. Remember, keep the content authentically helpful.

4. Host some Google hangouts. Hangouts are similar to webinars, but are done in real time and through video. Read the video chapter in this book if you need more detail on live streaming video.

5. If you have knowledge to provide and want to make some extra money, check out Google helpouts. These enable you to use the Google hangout technology and make some extra money (or use them as a lead generator).

6. Try to get those +1's. The more people that +1 your content and your posts, the better you will appear in the Google search engine results and the Google+ social network. Think of +1's as social proof.

LinkedIn

Why?

LinkedIn is gaining traction. The company has rolled out several new features and has seen a very nice spike in membership. This platform is focused on business networking. Posting content about what you ate for lunch will not fly. With that said, if you are looking to network with executives, this platform is amazing.

Who?

Anyone who is trying to reach people in the business-to-business space. There is no better platform than LinkedIn with reaching and connecting with business people.

How?

1. Complete your personal profile and optimize it for search. List the different skills you have so that if someone is looking for that service, you will come up on top.

2. Set up a LinkedIn business page for your business and encourage your customers and employees to join the business page. You can load up quite a bit of content on the page and is it widely underutilized by most.

3. My biggest tip with LinkedIn is to try to present your LinkedIn presence in a way that matches your offline world. In other words, your offline rolodex should look similar to what you put on LinkedIn.

4. Spend some money on Inmail. If you want to reach just about anyone on LinkedIn, you can pay for Inmail messages and make sure that your messages get delivered. Be sure to reply to messages, too. Inmail is a powerful way to connect.

5. Contribute to LinkedIn groups. Pick a few groups that you can make an active contribution to, and do so on a regular basis. I have often answered people's questions on LinkedIn only to get a message from someone asking for more information and a proposal or quote.

6. Connect with your customers and ask them to write a recommendation. The more recommendations you have on LinkedIn, the more respected you will appear.

Facebook

Why?

When people hear the term social networking, they often think of Facebook first. This is widely the largest social networking channel on the platform with an ever-growing number of members. They have a solid platform, a large number of features, and lots of things to keep all different audiences engaged and coming back for more.

Who?

Similar to YouTube.com, I can't think of any business that shouldn't look at marketing on Facebook. This is the first network I recommend starting on before moving onto other networks.

How?

1. Create a business page by going to Facebook.com/ pages. Select the category that makes the most sense for your business.

2. Build out the page with great content and some eye-catching graphics. Make sure that you conform to the size requirements for the backgrounds and profile pictures so you don't get pictures that end up getting cut off or that look quite strange.

3. Spend some money on Facebook ads to build up fan base. Read the content below on advertising. You can get to 1,000 targeted fans quite fast using something called Facebook custom audiences.

4. Provide great content on a daily (or more) basis. Posts with images perform much better than posts without images.

5. Engage with others across different fan pages and groups. Keep the content non-salesy and educational or helpful in nature.

6. Create Facebook-only specials for your product / service to keep people coming back often.

7. Look into using shortstack.com to create some very cool Facebook apps. You can have contests right on your fan page and lots of very nice-looking opt-in forms.

Twitter

Why?

At the time of writing, Twitter is the second most popular social network. The thing that is great about this platform is that messages don't take much time to craft (140 characters or less), so it is often the platform of choice for people to post on and get a quick news update on without having to read long drawn-out pieces of content.

Who?

I like this platform for ~~marketers who have 20 or so minutes a day to engage with people and send messages~~. There are very few businesses that Twitter doesn't make sense for—a funeral home may be tough on here, for example.

How?

1. Build your simplified biography and use a great-looking background and main image that is the proper size specifications.

2. Use search.twitter.com to look for topics that are currently active on Twitter and engage with people. Join in their conversions. If you are a business coach, you can look for anyone talking about having hiring challenges and write something helpful that they would enjoy. This will lead to your tweets getting marked as favorites, and targeted Twitter followers will link up with you.

3. Post content on a regular basis and use hashtags that make sense. If you can join in a trending hashtag, that's even better.

4. Test the waters with some Twitter-only specials.

5. Finally, look at the Twitter advertising platform. There is a lot of low-hanging opportunity there.

I included #business, because it was a trending topic at the time of this tweet. When you use a hashtag that's trending, you have a substantially better chance of getting engagement from people who aren't your followers. The couple of hundred people who click that hashtag every hour around the world might also see it, and I might get some traction I might not have otherwise received. I also made my tweet a question, because it makes your brain think about the answer. If I can get someone to stop for half a second to ponder, I've got him in my ecosystem. Also, line breaks allow your tweet to take up a larger portion of the phone screen and attract attention.

Pinterest

Why?

Pinterest is the first social commerce platform. What I mean by that is simple: People are coming to Pinterest to look for things to buy!

Who?

If you have a product or service that lends itself well to something visual, Pinterest is the place to be.

How?

1. Deck out your profile with some amazing graphics. Because Pinterest focuses on images, you must have really good stuff.

2. Create a few different pin boards to fill up your board. For example, if you sell furniture, you can have different boards for the different types of furniture, boards showing different living room setups, and even boards by price points. Don't forget to use hashtags so people can find your content easily.

3. To kick-start the party, you can pin some content from other people as they will often then do the same for you.

4. The secret to Pinterest is you want to be the one creating the great graphics, infographics, and the like so that others are pinning your stuff versus the other way around.

5. Find good quotes and pin it as text to convert text into images in seconds.

6. Add "permission to pin" buttons across your different graphics on your blog and web site so people know its okay to pin your content.

7. Do not forget a call to action on your pins (the ones that make sense).

8. Play with Pinterest contests (such as pin it to win it).

There are lots of other social networking channels out there. Here are three others to keep your eyes on:

- **Instagram.com (owned by Facebook).** This is an app-based network that allows you to upload pictures (and videos) and use hashtags for easier locating. It focuses on "real" images. For example, where are you now, what are you currently doing?

- **Vine.com.** This is another app-based network that focuses on short videos (6.5 seconds long). You can tell a story, do a product tease, or do a fun time lapse video, for example.

- **Tumblr.com.** This is a cross between a blog and Twitter. It is a streaming scrapbook of text content, photos, and even video or audio. Users can create or follow "tumblelogs" that can be opened to the public.

Social Media Disaster Planning

One of the reasons some business owners are worried about getting into social media marketing in the first place is because they are afraid their prospects and customers might leave negative feedback or comments on their profiles. Here is the truth of the matter: People are already talking about you—you just don't know about it. I would much rather be able to take part in the conversion versus the conversion happening behind my back.

So what do you do when disaster strikes? Depending on your definition of disaster, it can be something as small as a customer complaining about your service on their social media profile to something like your credit union getting robbed and thousands of messages being posted across all the major social media platforms.

The key with social media management is to monitor the conversations that are taking place and to reply in real time. The real-time piece is critical, but how you reply is even more critical. Own up if you make a mistake when participating in these conversations and offer some way to rectify potentially negative situations. The faster you reply, the better because all of the friends and followers of those viewing your response will see it and they will see that you are trying to make the situation right.

All people want is to be heard and responded to, quickly. If you are on hold on the telephone with customer service at a company you want to complain to (let's say the slow speed and high cost of your Internet), do you get happier or madder as time passes by while on hold?

Reply in real time, give a human response, and make the situation right, and you will be rewarded handsomely!

Social Media Advertising

In some of my recent speaking engagements, I have said that social media advertising is the modern day gold rush. I firmly believe that to be a true statement. I am doing amazing things with social media advertising while you are reading this very section and I want you to jump on the bullet train.

I love Google and pay-per-click marketing. But take a look at these two scenarios from a targeting perspective.

Let us say you are in the dog grooming business in Peoria, Illinois (my old college town).

- **Option #1:** Run a Google Adwords ad promoting your dog grooming business to people in and around Peoria. Use specific keywords such a "dog grooming."
- **Option #2:** Run an ad on a social network like Facebook promoting your dog grooming business to people in and around people who own a specific breed of a dog and have ample disposable income.

Both options are good, but 90% of the time I am going to lean on option two as I want to laser target a specific audience that is most likely to buy my product or service.

Social networks have a lot of personal information about us (age, location, interests, behaviors, and a whole lot more). That data becomes *very* useful for marketers like us who are looking to target specific people.

What I also really like about social media advertising is the ability to test a variety of different photos, headlines, ads, and landing pages for pennies on the dollar.

Tas Tip

You must keep in mind that people are not on social networks to be sold. They are coming on these networks to post pictures of their kids, view photos of friends, and waste time. The best ads are those that blend in with the content (called native advertising). A good native ad for a dog grooming business could be something like "The Six Secrets to Keeping Your Dog Healthy." When someone clicks on that link, it takes them to a landing page with the six secrets and a lot of information about your dog grooming services.

Here is how you can get started with social media advertising:

- Pick one platform to start with. I highly recommend you start with Facebook as it is the most advanced and has some powerful features (such as behavior targeting).

- Craft a compelling headline and ad. Start with one ad, and then look at testing other variations.

- Locate some eye-catching graphics that will stand out and catch people's attention. There are lots of free places to use, but I prefer to use high-end graphics. You can get a subscription on a web site such as Shutter Stock's for around $200 a month and download over 700 images in the month.

- Design a landing page that goes along with the flow and design of the ad and the picture. In a perfect world, people realize they are going to a totally new web site. You want things to blend so the user experience holds true.

- Start with a small or modest budget. I like to start testing an ad with about $25–$50/day. All the different platforms have different budget capacities and ways to test. I like to focus on something called "optimized cost for conversions." This allows Facebook to optimize my spending based on conversions (sales). You simply install a tracking code on the thank you page of the conversion to track a lead or a sale, for example. You can also advertise for clicks, advertise for Facebook fan likes or simply impressions (views).

- Test, test, and test. Quite quickly you will find out which of your photos and ads are working the best. Eliminate the others and then make more ads that are similar to the one that was working the best. This process should be a never ending battle as things can always be improved. You should be testing different headlines.

Case Study

Educators Credit Union is one of the best credit unions across the U.S. It does amazing things for its members and is growing at a rapid rate.

The company has an active Facebook fan page and wants it to be more active.

Through the power of Facebook, custom audiences, and some great copy, Educators Credit Union doubled the number of fans on its Facebook Page in less than 90 days!

Following are tips for getting started with social media from Educators Credit Union:

- Pick one platform to focus on and dominate that platform. Do not add another social media platform to the mix until you have the bandwidth to do so.

- Plan an editorial calendar for 30 days in advance. This will allow you to make sure you have content that is planned and organized.

- Find great images using companies like Shutter Stock. Almost every social marketing channel encourages graphics.

- Set up analytics to track your progress. Don't get discouraged because you feel you can't track your social marketing efforts. Set up landing pages, unique phone numbers, and even coupon codes so you can track the dollars to your business.

- Automate postings as it makes sense. Use a tool like Hootsuite.com to make this happen. This will then free your time up to focus on engaging with people in real time.

- Monitor your brand and conversations that include you. Make sure to jump on and clean things up (if needed) as soon as possible, or thank the person(s) for the compliments.

- Find a way to make the platform unique. If you have six different networks, treat each one differently and have specials for that network only.

- Be authentic!

Social media marketing is a trend that is only going to get stronger. Don't get bogged down in all the details and overwhelmed with the number of platforms. Pick one platform, dominate it, and then add a second platform when you have extra bandwidth. Keep things real and remember to be authentic. I promise you that your time on social media will be well spent and the dividends will start to pour in.

4

The Content Craze: Grabbing Your Customers' Attention Before Your Competition

For five years in a row, I sent out a yearly email to all of my clients that gave a summary of how the year looked (from a digital marketing standpoint), and what hot trends I saw coming up for the year. For each of the five years, the summary started with something that went like this, "The most profitable source of business for our clients came from content marketing this year, and we see that trend continuing strong." That statement still holds true today and it's one statement that I honestly don't see changing ever.

Can you imagine a time when you wouldn't want to get educated about a potential product or service you are considering purchasing or a time when you won't want to get educated about things in general? I don't know of too many people (if anyone) who would say something such as, "My brain is full. I have no need to learn more."

The way we learn is through experiences, reading, watching, or listening to other people. Let's say, for example, that you are looking at putting in an in-ground pool. Depending on your style for purchasing, you will most likely go to your network of friends (via social media) and say, "Does anyone know of any good pool contractors?" Armed with that information, you will call for a few of the contractors, get some quotes, and make a decision. The quoting process is among the best places for a contractor to set himself apart from the competition. The fact is, most consumers do not make purchasing decisions on price alone. They take the whole experience into consideration and look at things like trust, confidence in the business, feelings from the interaction with the salesperson, the perceived benefits, and any extra bonuses or special offers.

The way you set yourself apart from the first interaction all the way past the sale (and after) is by educating your prospects. The objective is to provide them a lot of great education in various mediums: handouts, graphics, charts, a blog, and a DVD just to name a few.

The content you put out has to be noteworthy. Do not throw together junk content and expect it to drive sales for you. In fact, it will most likely do the opposite. Post nothing at all rather than use subpar content. With the number of people publishing on the Web today, you have to make sure the content you distribute is solid, useful, educational content.

The objective of this chapter is to show you how to reach your customers *before* they check out your competition. We want to give them the content they are looking for at the right time and in the right medium. The mediums we focus on in this chapter are blogs, infographics, and podcasts.

Blogging

My favorite way for getting quality, targeted traffic on a consistent basis is through blogging. This is the strategy that I put quite a bit of my marketing dollars and personal energy toward. There was a time when the popularity of blogs dipped just a bit, but then they bounced back in popularity and seemed to skyrocket.

Blogging: What Is a Blog?

A *blog* is simply a web site that is a compilation of ideas, thoughts, events, photos, or other content-based information that the author of the blog is interested in sharing. People started blogging in 1999 and, due to the ease of deployment and use, the relatively low cost, and the ability to reach a wide audience, they have been increasing in popularity ever since. Blogs are composed of text content, videos, pictures, infographics, and more. Over 50 percent of the web sites on the Internet today *still* do not have any type of blog. If you don't have a blog, you are missing out on traffic. Blogs are a great way of developing a following, starting a cultural trend or movement, establishing yourself and your business as an expert, landing a book deal, and paying yourself through ad sales to indulge in your favorite expensive hobby. All in all, though, blogs are the best way to appease and get the attention of Google, which then gets the attention of your prospects through their searches.

The top blog systems are WordPress, Blogger, TypePad, Tumblr, and SquareSpace. WordPress has the majority of the market share due to the vast amount of add-ons available. It's said that nearly 1 in 6 web sites on the Internet is powered by WordPress.

Your Entire Web Site as a Blog

The top questions I get asked are, "Where should I host my blog? Should it be a different URL or be on my web site?" While you will find lots of conflicting information out there, the reason you are reading this book is for proven strategies that work. What works best is to make your entire site a blog and have the URL be something like yourdomain.com/blog. The only platform that I have recommended over the last few years for designing a web site is WordPress. Developing your web site on WordPress enables you to then integrate blog posts throughout the homepage and on the various inner pages. Instead reading boring "about us" content, consumers can read your educational blog posts.

If you have a full-blown e-commerce web site, I recommend using a different platform for the site, but still installing a WordPress blog on the web site. You will learn more about web site design throughout the book, but I wanted to debunk the top question I get asked that tends to stop people in their tracks. Don't overthink this too much. Instead, act. Action will drive the results.

The Two Key Types of Blogs

The two primary types of blogs are personal blogs and corporate/business blogs. There are other variations, but these are the main two that you see the most often:

- **Personal:** These blogs are the most popular in nature because they can be on any topic, including family, hobbies, sports, school, other interests, or even just emphatic opinions. It seems that people who post blogs on the Web ranting and raving about a product, a service, the latest movie, or someone in their social circle gain the most attention. Don't be afraid of offending readers—assuming, of course, that you believe in the opinion you're promoting. Let's face it: Controversy sells.
- **Corporate/Business:** Interested in promoting your products or services while building a relationship with your customers and prospects? Corporate blogs are a great tool for this task. Almost all the Fortune 1,000

companies maintain at least one public blog. The content typically is a mix between promotion of their offerings and some public relations content that is offered as a way to further build loyalty. This may range from photos of the executives having fun in the office, to customer testimonials, or even photos of employees' pets.

Other types of blogs include political, charity, media, and social blogs.

There are two other web sites that are a mix between a blog and other elements that need to be mentioned. The first site is Squidoo. You can log onto Squidoo by going to www.Squidoo.com. This platform is the brainchild of legendary marketer Seth Godin. On Squidoo, authors create what they refer to as "lens." Their current catch phrase is millions of useful, fun pages built by real people, like you. I always love to see both the words fun and useful in a sentence.

The second platform is Medium.com. This platform is built for both readers and writers. Among its main draw is the nice writing interface combined with the ability to make comments on specific pieces of text versus making a comment on the entire article as a whole. It is simplistic in nature and for some industries, it has proven to drive a quality flow of content. The secret is to align yourself with some of the other bloggers on the platform, allowing your ideas get spread much faster.

While I would not look at using Squidoo.com or Medium.com as your main blogging platform and tool, they make great add-ons after you have gained traction on your main blog. Pay close attention to that last phrase, "once you have gained traction." The kiss of death with a blog is to not update it on a regular basis. Don't spread yourself too thin by getting on every platform I recommend. Instead, add more platforms and more marketing tactics when the time to do so makes sense.

Why Should You Be Blogging?

Blogs grow your visibility—and therefore enhance your marketing efforts. Search engines *LOVE* blogs because of their content-based nature.

Blogs are also one of the best places to start building (or, expanding on) relationships. This should be considered an extension to your sales process. Most companies don't have enough resources to call on customers or prospects every day, but can easily "touch them" through this medium. Give them good content, and they will keep coming back for more. The notion that content is king on the Web stands and will continue to stand as I mentioned in the introduction. The more original content you provide, the better. Good content provides readers with useful information.

How to Fully Utilize the Power of Your Blog

Many companies or individuals start blogs and update those only two or three times a month, if that. The biggest thing I can share with you on blogging is that you want to aim to update it at least three to five times each and every week. The updates can be long articles with great information, shorter articles, a video, an audio, a photo, and even simply a random thought with a link.

I recommend that everyone utilize a blog as a marketing tool. The simple rationale: Google and the various search engines love blog content. Because of this, your blog will start ranking in the top of the search engines for different keywords and tags that you select for your content.

When most business leaders hear they should be updating their blog several times a week, they panic. This doesn't mean you need to log in and post every day. Get into the habit of batching your posts a few times each week and schedule them out to post in advance—a wonderful feature of blogging. Again, keep in mind that these posts do not always need to be long articles. It's best to provide useful content or tools to your blog readers, but random thoughts have also been well received. Frequency of posting is much more critical than the length of the content.

Get people excited about coming to your blog often. You do this by blowing them away with amazing content and special offers just for them.

Here are a few interesting blogs worth checking out. These have all done a great job at getting their blogs noticed and have built a very large following of readers:

- **www.theminimalists.com:** This blog is about living a minimalist life.

- **www.lifehacker.com:** This blog talks about all things "hacking" your life.

- **www.diy.org:** This blog teaches you about doing things yourself.

- **www.nojokemarketing.com/blog:** Of course I had to put my marketing training blog in there!

These blogs focus on providing educational, actionable content.

Because consumers have less and less time, I recommend you keep your posts short and to the point. Normally, readers won't read 3,000–5,000 words in a posts unless they are highly engaging. The blog length I tend to recommend is 300–500 words for written content, and videos that are under three minutes in length. Content such as five things you need to know about creating a greener home, the three keys to a successful marriage, or the best five stocks to buy now and why makes great headlines. Keep your information tight, and you will maintain loyal readers.

One other hidden benefit from blogging is people who subscribe to your RSS feed. When someone provides an email address, he is asking to be notified every time a new blog post goes live. When compared to email marketing, an RSS feed notification is seen as much less spammy and often gets opened and read more often. Not only do you get to capture new subscribers, but you get to notify them each time you post an update.

Plug-ins (or, add-ons) allow you to customize your blog. Some of the add-ons aid in providing technical help or details to remove spam and provide stats. Others help your readers stay in touch with you or follow you more easily. Blogs cannot go without plug-ins being used—they are just too powerful.

As the names and versions of plug-ins can change quickly, I will provide more general information. The way to then lock in on the best plug-in is to simply search for the topic in the WordPress plug-in directory and sort by ratings. If the plug-in has a poor rating, don't install it. Here are some of the types of plug-ins you want to get installed on your blog:

- **SEO:** An amazing plug-in that makes your blog posts much more search-engine friendly.

- **Spam blocking:** A tool to help eliminate all the spam posts.

- **RSS feeds/feed burner:** A live RSS feed for anyone who prefers to use feeds to get their updates.

- **Social Sharing:** This plug-in is critical as it allows viewers to easily share your content.

- **Social tagging:** The ability for readers to tag the different blog posts.

- **Google sitemaps:** A tool to help Google index the blog more easily.

- **Featured Images:** A tool that allows you to set a nice featured image.

- **Podcasting:** A tool that allows people to listen to audios as podcasts.

- **Related posts:** This shows posts that are related to the one you are reading.

Tas Tip

Visit www.marketinginthemomentbook.com/plugins to find more of the top plug-ins.

Checklist: *Blogging*

Check off the steps as you go, so you make sure you've covered everything!

❑ Decide which type of blog platform you want to use: www.WordPress.com, www.Blogger.com, www.TypePad.com, www.Tumblr.com, or www.SquareSpace.com.

❑ Hire a designer to make your blog match your brand. Depending on your situation, in a perfect world, your blog will be integrated throughout the web site. If you need to start elsewhere, get the blog added as a link to your web site using one of the previous platforms.

❑ Trick out your blog with all the latest and greatest plug-ins.

❑ Add an RSS feed and a place for people to opt-in to your Web site.

❑ Start adding quality content to the blog in written, audio, and video form.

❑ Make sure your content is tagged with proper keywords (using the SEO plug-in).

❑ Submit each post to various social-bookmarking sites. www.SocialMarker.com is a great free tool to accomplish this task quickly.

❑ Monitor your analytics to see which posts are getting the most visits and comments, and put out more content around that topic. Give the people what they are looking for!

- ❑ Email your mailing list asking people to leave comments on your blog. This gets the community interaction flowing.
- ❑ Keep your blog updated often. Our recommendation is three to five posts per week.

Case Study

Randy wanted to become the top real-estate agent in Tampa, Florida. He set up a web site and started doing some social marketing, SEO, and link building, but he was not getting much traction. His web site was averaging only about 10 visits per day, or about 300 each month. We (Taz Solutions, Inc.) set him up a rocking WordPress blog with the focus of educating the marketplace rather than being in their face 24/7 and constantly selling. His web site was focused on promoting his current listings and generating his new listings. But the blog also shared useful information, including the best places to eat in Tampa, the ratings of the various school districts, and the advantages of living in Tampa versus other places in the United States.

The Result: In three weeks, Randy's blog was averaging 175 unique visits per day. His listings increased by 25%, and his properties started selling faster than those of any other agents in his office.

The Takeaway: A blog combined with some great content can produce results very quickly.

Infographics

As we have become more of a visual society, infographics have risen in popularity. Some of the most shared and most viewed content on the Internet today are infographics, thanks in large part to social networking.

Infographics: What Are They?

An *infographic* is simply a visual image such as a chart or diagram that is used to represent information or data. One of the most common infographics (that you probably didn't realize was an infographic) is the weather report you see in newspapers. They can also be used to present complex information in a much more organized fashion. The old saying a picture is worth a thousand words holds true for infographics.

There are all types of statistics online about why infographics work. One of the most compelling statistics is that 65 percent of us are visual learners. For those of us in that category, we are much more likely to take action and process the information when presented an infographic versus just words on a page.

Marketing with Infographics

The first and most important step with infographics is to produce content that will lend itself to being shared and content that people want. Similar to blog content, your infographic content should be useful, thought-provoking, it should make sense for your business, and it should be fun. If you start with content that doesn't lend itself to one of these mantras, you may end up spinning your wheels a bit.

Brainstorm a list of potential infographics based on content you already have in-house, or content you can easily create. Then locate some useable statistics to complement the infographic. Please don't get me wrong, you don't need to use statistics on the entire infographics, but statistics breed credibility and credibility leads to sharing.

Armed with the content you choose to use, the next step is the design process. This step can take on one of many different directions. The first option is to tackle the project in-house. If you have creative graphic designers on staff, they are always the best option because they know your brand.

Another option is to leverage one of the many infographic creation tools out there to make the process a bit easier. These tools use pre-made templates and allow you to fill in your information.

A few of the ones I recommend are the following:

- Infogr.am
- InfoActive
- Piktochart
- Easel.ly
- Visual.ly

The advantage of using one of the tools mentioned here is speed. You can typically create a visually appealing infographic in under 30 minutes, whereas if you are starting from scratch, the process will take hours, even potentially days.

The third option is to simply outsource the infographic to a designer on one of the big freelance web sites, even Fiverr.com. Yes, for $5, you can have your very own infographic.

The test I use to determine what route I'm going to take is simple. If the infographic I'm putting out there has the potential to be viewed by thousands of people, I do it in-house or hire a professional. If the infographic is going to be leveraged internally or for a small random side project, I'll get something quick on Fiverr.com. You would be surprised the quality you can still achieve for five dollars, but know that it will not be a "from scratch" project. At that price, software and templates are used to create it.

During the design process, you want to pay attention to the flow of the infographic. Don't present information overload. Make sure your graphics are visually appealing, and in a perfect world, you will tell a story with the infographic.

Among the most important elements at the bottom (or top) of the infographic is your call to action. Don't forget to include some type of call to action on your content along with a standard copyright notice. Because this is an educational piece of content, the best call to action is to provide more free content. For example, you may have a video that complements the infographic and viewers simply have to provide an email address to get it.

Finally, leverage the other strategies presented in this book to get as much traction from your infographic as possible. Share it on your blog, on social media, and various news sites. Make sure you share the infographic and make it easy for others to do the same.

Podcasting

Every now and then there are some marketing trends and tactics that tend to take a dive (such as blogging), but then spike back with a vengeance. Podcasting is another one of those tactics. With the continued growth of mobile devices, podcasting is back in action and proving to be a great way to generate awareness and business.

What Is Podcasting?

Podcasting is the practice of creating audio files and making them available to the public. Normally speaking, podcasts are done in a series—whether it is on a certain topic or a regular frequency—often morphing into a web radio-like show.

How to Get Started

With any type of content creation, the most important element is figuring out the content that will get created. Although content that is educational in nature works well, fun and upbeat content works just as well. If you start to think about this as more of a show versus just publishing audio content, your content will become more interesting. What works well is establishing a regular schedule for publication. For example, every Tuesday at 10:00AM, a new podcast gets published (more on this soon). This allows your listeners to have something to look forward to and keeps you on a schedule.

Depending on the style of the person who produces the content and the nature of your business, you can take one of many approaches for the tone of the podcast. Some people do well off the cuff and are at their best with simply a few notes jotted down. Others need everything scripted out, so that nothing is forgotten. A balance of the two seems to work the best. I recommend that you script out any key language that is needed (such as the introduction or calls to action) and have talking points for the rest. When you are listening to the podcast, the last thing you want is for these to sound boring and dry, or as if you are simply reading from a teleprompter.

In terms of the format for your podcast, a variety of things work well, including the following:

- Weekly (or daily) updates or new content
- Guest appearances and interviews
- Question and answer sessions
- Reviews or critiques
- Short training snippets

A common question is, "How long should these be?" The answer depends on a host of different factors, but aim for the 30-minute mark. I started No Joke Marketing weekly and have aimed to be in the 30-minute range. Sometimes, I go over, sometimes I'm under, but for marketing types of training, that time frame works well.

On the flip side, certain businesses lend themselves to keeping things short and simple. It depends on your business and your listeners. You also don't have to follow the exact same format each week. The idea is to test the waters and get feedback. Let your listeners dictate the content they find most enjoyable.

If you are going to do this on a regular basis, you should come up with a name for your show and hire someone to do a nice voice introduction. This adds a huge amount of credibility and also makes it more enjoyable for your listeners. It's said that listeners build a unique relationship with radio show hosts that they listen to on a regular basis. You want to create the same magic here. My favorite site for getting voice talent is voices.com. For about $100, you can have a professional introduction recorded with music.

Armed with some content ideas, a name for your show, and a professionally recorded introduction, you are ready to buy some equipment.

The Technology and Devices Needed

Depending on how serious you are going to get with podcasting, you can start off on the cheaper side and then buy equipment that is more expensive. I recommend that people start off with middle-of-the-road technology first and see how things go. The great thing about podcasting is that even the high-end technology isn't expensive.

The most important piece in your tool kit is your microphone. If your audio comes out distorted, you will have a hard time attracting people to your podcast. If you want to keep things simple, you can use a microphone that plugs directly into a USB port on your PC or Mac. I'm a fan of Blue Microphone (the snowball) and have several of them.

On the more expensive side, you can look at purchasing higher end microphones, such as a Behringe. These setups become much more advanced and of course much more expensive.

There are literally thousands of different microphones to choose from. I've done well with those under $100 and those that can fit in my luggage, so I can create podcasts from the road.

Many microphones can sit right on your desk, but others need a stand. A pop filter is also a nice edition to your tool kit, helping to prevent the popping sound from certain words.

Once you have your microphone rolling, the last piece of equipment you need is the software to do the actual recording.

Here is a list of the most popular tools (many of which you may already own):

- Sound recorder (installed on PCs)
- Garage Band (installed on Macs)
- Audacity
- Camtasia
- Pro Tools

These tools make the assumption that you are recording in your location. If you want to bring on a guest who is not sitting with you, you can leverage tools such as Google Hangouts, Skype, Go To Meeting, HotRecorder.com, or even a simple phone bridge line. The key is to make sure the person you are interviewing also has a good audio setup and a fast Internet connection; otherwise, you are going to hear them cutting in and out and that does not bode well with your listeners.

Recording Your First Podcast

After you have your devices set up, hit record and conduct your first podcast. If you make a few mistakes along the way, don't worry. If you botch something completely, I recommend starting from scratch and doing it again. The good thing is this isn't live radio. If you make mistakes, you can start over or edit the mistake out.

Make sure you stay upbeat. Keep the content moving, so dead air is minimized. Remember that fun can go a long way here.

Once you have the recording completed, you can leverage your software tool to do some light editing (such as balancing the sound). Just make sure to include the introduction you had recorded.

Distributing Your Podcast

Now that you have your final file, you can move onto the distribution piece. This can get a bit technical, but I want to give you a good overview so you can take the needed action yourself, or get someone to assist.

Once the file is on your computer, let's say it's called podcast1.mp3. You need to add some information about this specific piece of audio before it gets uploaded. This is called tagging. The technical piece involves editing the metadata or ID3 tags. You need to include this information with your file so the various media players can comprehend and display things such as the title for your podcast, your name, the show number, or even the artwork for the podcast.

Once the podcast is tagged, you need to upload it and store it on a server somewhere so whenever a media player (or outlet) wants to play it (such as iTunes), it knows where to grab the audio file from. I recommend using Amazon S3, but you can also use other tools such as www.podbean.com, www.buzzsprout.com, or www.soundcloud.com.

Now that the file is uploaded to a server, you will get a link that points directly to your audio file. This link is important because it is the place that the media players and various directions use to play your podcast.

The trickiest piece is the final piece and that is to set up a feed. A feed is a way to syndicate content so it is easier to read by various web sites, applications and directories. In the beginning of this chapter, I talked about loving WordPress. If you take that advice, you will already be set up with a feed and just need to do some simple tweaking.

Podcast directories, such as iTunes, Sticher, and Zune, will read the feed, know a new show came out, and post your content. The beautiful thing is that after you set up the feed once, all you need to do is keep publishing podcasts directly to your web site and iTunes and the various other directories automatically get updated.

How to Get Thousands of Listeners

Now that you have done all the hard work, you might be thinking, so how do I get lots of listeners? The shortest way is to produce great content on a regular basis. If you produce good content, people will talk, people will give you a great rating, and people will blog about you. The great thing with iTunes is that your podcast will be available for free, encouraging even more listeners.

The other ways to get your podcast heard by more people is to promote it via other channels. Write blog posts about your podcasts, do a press release or two, promote it across social media, send an email blast to your list. Often a show starts out with just a handful of listeners and grows like wildfire due to the content. Podcasts are easy to share across the web and your happy listeners will eagerly do the work for you.

Checklist: Podcasting

Check off the steps as you go, so you make sure you've covered everything!

- ❏ Decide on the nature of the content you will be producing, and remember that fun, actionable content works well.
- ❏ Create a name for your show and artwork to match.
- ❏ Hire a professional to do a great introduction using something like www.voices.com.
- ❏ Buy the needed microphone, equipment, and software.
- ❏ Record your first podcast.
- ❏ Put the introduction ahead of your podcast and make it into one file, saving it to your desktop.
- ❏ Tag the audio file correctly so the media players know what to call it.
- ❏ Upload the audio to a server (where it will be hosted).
- ❏ Create a feed on your web site so the podcast directories can grab the file from the server.
- ❏ Spread the word across other channels to grow your following.

5

Mobile Marketing: The One Trend That Cannot Be Ignored

In the first edition of this book, I focused quite a bit on mobile marketing and called it my favorite tactic, saying, "Get in on the ground floor." Had you followed that advice, receiving it would have been like insider trading as few businesses practiced mobile marketing at the time. What is surprising to me, however, is if we fast forward four years to now. What you will discover is that there is still a lot of gold to be mined. It's hard to go more than a day without hearing about the mobile revolution, but for whatever reason, marketers and businesses alike have been slow to adapt to these changes.

Mobile is the one trend that cannot be ignored. Mobile devices are replacing computers. In many countries, there are more mobile phones than people—the United States, Russia, Hong Kong, and Brazil to name a few. Countries that were deemed "third world" are starting to do business via mobile phones. Everywhere you look, people are glued to their phones. Ever hear of second screen syndrome? Many people watch television while browsing their phone at the same time. If you take away nothing else from this book (which would not be a good thing), please take away this: Adopt mobile marketing and your business will prosper.

What Is Mobile Marketing?

When I refer to mobile marketing in this book, I'm referring to marketing to or on a mobile device, such as receiving a text message from a vendor with a promotional code, buying products right from your phone, or viewing picture messages that depict a product you may be interested in. In general, anything that has to do with a mobile device can be considered mobile marketing.

There are various marketing methods with mobile phones, the most popular being SMS, or short messaging service (text messages). Other forms of mobile marketing include MMS (multimedia messaging service), in-game marketing, mobile apps, and mobile responsive web sites. Not only do you want to engage with your customers and prospects, but you also want to be certain any interaction they have with your business via their mobile device is a pleasurable experience.

Mobile Marketing with SMS

When people hear mobile marketing, they typically think of text messages. Let's start with the most popular method: SMS.

Marketing on a mobile phone has become much more popular since the rise of SMS, or short message service. This rise began in the early 2000s in Europe and parts of Asia when businesses started to gather mobile phone numbers of consumers. With these mobile numbers in hand, they started blasting out content (whether people requested the content or not). What they found was that this really was a channel with some major legs to grow and expand. Surprisingly, consumers were actually happy to receive text messages from businesses they had visited. This eliminated the whole permission marketing constraint because very few people objected. In fact, many who didn't receive the text messages felt left out and wanted to join the list!

In the past few years, SMS marketing has become a much more accepted advertising channel, but one that few smaller- to medium-sized businesses use. One of the many reasons SMS, or mobile marketing in general, has started to become accepted into society is that it's policed much more than email. The carriers (Verizon, AT&T, Sprint, and so on), who watch over their networks, have set guidelines and precedents for the mobile-marketing industry. Open your email inbox and look at how many spam messages you have. In the past 24 hours, I have received 552 spam emails. Although there have been lots of new regulations to combat spam (for example, the Canadian spam laws that require heavy consent), email marketing is still quite abused. Take a look at your mobile device. How many spam messages do you have in your text messaging inbox? I have zero.

As SMS marketing continued to grow, the mobile community wanted to come up with another way to simplify the communication. Over the past few years, mobile short codes have been increasingly popular as a new channel to communicate with the mobile consumer. Businesses have started to treat the mobile short code as a type of mobile domain name allowing consumers to text a message at an event, in the store, or right off their packaging. For example, Verizon Wireless tends to run different promotions allowing customers to send a text message to receive a percentage off their next purchase. They have various signs in their stores, so while you're waiting, why not grab a mobile coupon code?

SMS services normally run off a short code, but sending text messages to an email address is another tactic. These codes are five- or six-digit numbers that have been assigned by all the mobile operators in a given country for the use of brand campaigns and other consumer services.

So the gist of mobile marketing through SMS is two-fold:

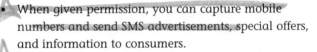

- When given permission, you can capture mobile numbers and send SMS advertisements, special offers, and information to consumers.
- Short codes can be used for various types of promotions.

Mobile Marketing with MMS (Pictures/Videos)

MMS stands for multimedia messaging service, a telecommunications standard for sending messages that include multimedia objects such as images, audio, video, and rich text. When I think of MMS, I think of picture messaging. When it comes down to it, MMS is simply an extension of SMS. All phones that have a color screen have the capability to send and receive MMS messages.

There are various cool marketing uses for MMS. One example is at the House of Blues. The brand allows visitors to send their mobile photos to the LED board, and then House of Blues staffers blog about the various images online.

MMS marketing can help in all areas, from increasing brand recognition to more sales, deeper interactivity, and increasing event attendance.

As many people say, a picture is worth a thousand words. If you have a product or service that is visually appealing, it makes a lot of sense to send an MMS message.

Due to the size that videos have to be when being sent as an MMS, I recommend you focus more of your efforts on compelling pictures, but sending a MMS message that contains a video can also be tested. Let's say the company you work for is a credit union and you want to do a unique onboarding campaign. Why not send a video welcome message from the president or CEO?

In-Game Mobile Marketing

Mobile users are starting to play video games across their phones in real time with other users. This is similar to people being able to play games against each other using a video game system like PlayStation or Xbox. Gamers are finding an increasing number of sponsored ads across some of these games produced for mobile devices. If your target audience might be playing games, find the various games they frequent and contact the advertising department to see what the different rates are. In a perfect world, you will pay only for clicks on your ad rather than a flat rate.

Mobile Web Marketing

The standard term *mobile Web marketing*, in this instance, refers to placing ads on the mobile Web, very similar to the ads you see when browsing Google or Yahoo!. The Mobile Marketing Association does provide a set of guidelines and standards giving the recommended format of ads, presentation, and metrics used in reporting. Google, Yahoo!, and other content providers that have been selling advertising placement for years are now shifting to mobile-ad placement, and it's really starting to catch on.

Mobile Marketing Guidelines

One of the biggest advantages to mobile marketing is not only that the carriers are keeping an eye on the whole industry, but that the Mobile Marketing Association is quite active as well. The association is committed to helping advertisers make more money using mobile marketing while helping protect consumers from being spammed.

These are the key guidelines of mobile marketing (according to the MMA):

- Consumers need to be a double opt-in and have the ability to opt out at any time (similar to email). Only they can decide whether they want to receive your information.

- Respecting consumer privacy should be your number-one concern. If this gets out of hand, mobile marketing will go right out the window.

- The information collected needs to be handled with the utmost concern to security and privacy and must be up to par with the laws of that location on handling customer data.

- If there is a contest or something of that nature, it should be explained so that consumers know if there are fees or other commitments on their part (certain language must be used).

- Marketing to anyone under the age of 13 brings up many ethical questions and is a major issue.

Marketers, who like to dance on the wild side, prefer limited regulation. In fact, the can-spam laws put tens of thousands of marketers out of business overnight and many in jail. With stricter regulations, consumers can get information they actually want or request, helping open rates, adoption rates, and sales. The few legitimate marketers in the industry who take the regulations and guidelines to heart are the ones here to stay. The fly-by-nightcompanies will continue to bite the dust.

A World Run on Mobile Devices

Take a look around when you're on the subway, at a conference, at a party, or even at a concert. Chances are, without trying, you'll spot everyone on their mobile devices.

There are more than 7 billion, yes that's *billion*, cellphone subscriptions in the world, as reported by MobiThinking. Growth is slowing a bit in developed countries with the largest expansion showing up in developing countries. Just think of the possibilities. Consumers are using their mobile phones to run their entire lives. They are texting like crazy, shopping from their phones, interacting with apps, and updating their social media statuses in real time.

Developing a Mobile Responsive Web Site

A few years ago, the trend was to grab a .mobi domain name and get a web site developed just for mobile. Unfortunately, with the ever so frequent changing of devices and screen sizes, this has become a challenging task. The new way is to design a web site that is 100 percent mobile responsive. This simply means that regardless of the device (a 4-inch mobile phone screen, or a 60-inch television), the web site will respond to those features and format itself automatically to look nice on those devices.

If your web site does not look good on a mobile device, it's time for a revamp. If a potential prospect is looking for information on your web site and is having issues on their mobile device, they are going to leave.

To Do: Designing a Mobile Responsive Web Site

Having a mobile responsive web site is critical to marketing survival. A responsive web site will ensure you do not lose any potential customers due to your web site not loading correctly on the device they are using at the time. Here are the steps for designing a mobile responsive web site:

Step 1.　Use MobileTest.me to see how your web site currently stacks up on a mobile device.

Step 2. Depending on the outcome of Step 1, you can either revamp your existing web site or start from scratch. This step can go into hundreds of different directions depending on the shape and size of your business. The coding language is HTML5, bootstrap, and CSS media query.

Step 3. If you decide to start with a mobile responsive framework from the beginning, I recommend locating a good template to start with and having a graphics team make graphics to customize the theme to your liking. Web sites such as ThemeForest.com and StudioPress.com are two great sources for mobile responsive templates that can be customized.

Because the bulk of the people reading this book are not programmers, I won't go into all the coding languages and things like that here, but the secret is that any additions or customizations made to the base theme should be checked on MobileTest.me to make sure they still look good on various mobile devices.

Step 4. Leverage Google's speed test tool on the developer web site (*https://developers.google.com/speed/pagespeed/insights/*) to see if you need to make any changes from a load standpoint.

Step 5. Continue to test and tweak your web site as needed if new elements are added.

How to Implement Mobile Marketing

Unlike many of the other tactics discussed in this book, mobile marketing has quite a few different angles. Some will apply to your business, others will not. But with mobile, pick a few, follow the how-to instructions, and implement.

SMS

SMS, or a text message, is one of the easiest ways to start gaining traction in the mobile marketing world. Text messages have a 95 percent to 100 percent open rate! In contrast, with email marketing, the highest open rate I have ever seen is 74 percent. But, sadly, the average open rate of an email is around 25 percent.

The other great thing about SMS marketing is that the messages are short, so they are typically read in full. You'd be smart to have a very specific, focused message in your text.

Keeping People Up-to-Date

Most businesses have some type of e-newsletter. But they may not be using their newsletter to its fullest advantage. Start collecting mobile numbers so you can send a short, every-now-and-then message about the happenings of your business and upcoming events.

Here's an example of a good message: Good Guys Pizza is celebrating its 5-year anniversary. Stop in for a free slice of pizza on Friday.

Special Offers

Need to announce a special product offering, a short promotion, or a discount code? With a very high open rate (and a short delay in opening), popping out specials to your mobile list through a text message will stir up some action!

Hold a Contest

"Submit your mobile number and be entered into a contest to win *(fill in a fantastic prize here)*." It's a great way to capture numbers in a nonthreatening way. Just make sure you have all your legal ducks in a row. Hosting a contest can get legally complicated, but it can bring in some great results. All of the big mobile marketing companies have the technology built in to allow for voting and different things like that.

Case Study

Instead of plugging in a case study here of how other companies have used text-messaging contests in their businesses, I want to include you in a contest we're having! When you bought this book, you automatically (with or without your knowing) got in line, if you will, for a free giveaway.

Go to www.marketinginthemomentbook.com to register. On this page, enter your mobile number, name, and email. A text is sent to your phone that tells you if you're the winner. Winner of what, you may be asking? We are giving away three high-end coaching/consulting packages absolutely free as a way of saying thank you for buying this book and participating in our contest!

Reminders

Text a short reminder for an upcoming event, promotion, or special you're offering—really anything for which you want to give your clients a friendly nudge/reminder.

Customer Service/Client Care

Consider a text message from a recent appointment or sale saying, "Thank you so much for your business; we can't wait to be able to serve you again soon!"? Wouldn't you love to get that type of message? I know I sure would. And to date, I have received a handful of these compared to the number of businesses that have my mobile phone number.

Interaction

The key to social marketing is the interaction and making people feel welcome and part of something. As opposed to always being one-way with your SMS marketing, try out some interaction. Allow people to send text messages with various requests, ideas, thoughts, questions, and comments. Take it a step further and allow people to vote on particular topics! I saved this one for last, because I feel it has the biggest impact. When you involve your prospects and customers, they grow to further know, like, and trust you and your business.

Case Study

Yankee Spirits Liquor is a small liquor store in my home town of North Tonawanda, New York. The company recently started deploying a mobile marketing campaign titled "Get the VIP treatment." It has QR codes in the store to sign up as well as a mobile short code. When you sign up, you get an instant discount on your purchase. Furthermore, during the month, Yankee Spirits Liquor sends special offers and promotions. Sending out the messages each month drives new people in the door as well as current customers in on a more frequent basis.

To Do: How to Get Started with Mobile Marketing

To get started with mobile marketing, follow these steps:

Step 1. Find a text-messaging company.

Sign up for a service that enables you to capture, send, and receive text messages in large quantities. Here are a few companies you can check out:

> www.trumpia.com
>
> www.mobilestorm.com
>
> www.sumotext.com
>
> www.eztexting.com
>
> www.mozeo.com

Some of these companies have one-time setup fees; for others, you can buy the license or even pay monthly fees based on your usage. Each of the companies has different product offerings. www. Trumpia.com, for example, has numerous additional offerings other than just mobile marketing. Check them out and search Google for other companies that offer similar services.

Step 2. Get mobile numbers!

Remember the statistics on how many people are carrying mobile phones? Chances are, 85 percent of people in your country will be carrying a mobile phone.

Start capturing mobile numbers instead of (or in addition to) land-line phone numbers. Here are eight ways to capture mobile numbers:

- Ask for mobile numbers everywhere.
- Let your customers and prospects know that they are part of an elite group who will be updated before anyone else (as long as this is true).
- Offer a free gift in exchange for their number.
- Ask people to refer a friend, providing their information as well, in exchange for a bonus or two.
- Host a contest; to enter, contestants simply submit their name and mobile number.
- Get them involved, allowing them to interact with you via text.
- Pay them cash.
- Reassure them that you won't be spamming them and that their information is kept secure, and watch your capture rates climb drastically.

Step 3. Decide which marketing tactics you are going to employ.

You can use a combination of them all. Keep in mind that it's important to stay mobile-compliant.

Step 4. Keep your lists segmented if possible.

Maintaining several different mobile phone lists allows you to further craft your messages to the exact target audience. Knowing who is using a smartphone versus who is not is also very powerful information. This allows you to craft messages with links for smartphone users and solely text messages for those who won't be able to view the link from their device.

Step 5. Construct your message carefully and effectively.

- Because you're limited on the numbers of characters you can use, you need to make certain that your language is effective, direct, and to the point, causing users to take your desired action.

  For example, 1-Day-Only Sale on All Jeans. 25% off when you mention the phrase "Blue Jeans." Expires at 10 PM.

- Play with your verbiage several times. Before I send any message via text, I do at least 7 rewrites. When doing a massive promotion, I've done as many as 40 drafts. Every word needs to be crafted for maximum impact.

- Use web site links selectively in case your prospects cannot view them on their particular phone. Use a service like www.TinyURL.com to make your links shorter, if they are long, to save on characters.

- Make sure you are providing information that is requested or that is of value, keeping in mind that many people still pay per text message.

Step 6. Send the message.

Step 7. Repeat.

Be careful with how many messages you send each month. You may have issues with negative responses to the frequency of two messages a week, for example. Two to four messages each month may be more reasonable.

MMS

SMS messages are great, but MMS takes things up another notch with color, sound, and all sorts of interesting action. There are six ways to integrate MMS marketing into your current tactics, which are covered in the following sections.

Special Offers/Discounts/Promotions

Special offers and discounts always seem to fare well in the mobile-marketing arena. Send a photo of an image that gives a special offer. To receive the offer, the recipient must either:

- Take action on the photo (visit a web site, or call a number).
- Bring a phone to the store and show the actual coupon to receive the discount or special offer.

Trumpia and some of the other bigger mobile solutions have something called mobile e-cards. This allows you to select from pre-existing graphics to send a fun card for a holiday or special occasion. Think about how fun it would be to send a mobile e-card on your prospects' (or customers') birthdays.

Case Study

Although this is an older case study, I am a huge fan of how it went. BMW has always prided itself on staying on the leading edge of innovation. It also prides itself on being masters at marketing—so much so, in fact, that the company has vowed to test and use all the different mobile-marketing tactics. In 2008, it wanted to push its newly released snow tires. To test the waters, it sent an MMS message to different lists showing what the car it owned (down to the specific model) would look like with the new snow tires. Customers could also download an application to see how the tires would look on various other cars.

The Result: BMW achieved a 30 percent conversion rate and rated this campaign as one of its most successful ever!

Video Clips/Animated Clips

I'm sure you have seen video clips floating around. Typically they are funny jokes or risqué clips. There are so many things you can do with video. Check these out:

- A thank-you-for-your-business video
- New-product announcement
- New-store opening
- Limited-time special
- Birthday video
- Super-client testimonial

The sky is the limit when it comes to video. Keep the videos short, inoffensive, amusing, content-rich, and worthwhile. Don't simply send videos for the sake of sending videos.

Interaction

As with SMS, you can get some fun interaction going with MMS. Allow people to send in videos they took with their phones. Turn a simple campaign into a contest and give away some cool prizes. Invite customers to give video testimonials about what it's like working with you or using your products. Have people send in video questions to be posted on your site, and answer them live. Keeping the interaction flowing will keep the dollars coming in!

Audio Clips

We love video, but we also love audio, because we're able to multitask while listening. It's much more challenging to multitask while watching a video. The audio clips can be informational, talking about specials, saying thank you, sending a birthday or holiday greeting, telling people where you are (a cool trip or great conference), and so on. It can be pretty much about anything you want.

How-To Information

Wouldn't it be great to get a short video or audio on how to use what you just purchased? This goes across all the different markets, from consumer goods to electronics to consumables and so much more. You walk into the store and pick up four high-end steaks, and two minutes later, you get an MMS message with instructions on the best way to prepare your dinner, and even suggested sides or wine. How-to information is well received in the marketplace. It makes for better customer relations as well as a solid opportunity for potential additional purchases.

 ## Freebies

Who doesn't love a good freebie? You can send free applications, pictures, videos, audios—anything of value.

To Do: How to Get Started Sending MMS Messages

To get started with sending MMS messages, follow these steps:

Step 1. Leverage MMS.

The solution you are leveraging for SMS marketing should also have the capability to send MMS messages.

Step 2. Tailor your content and approach.

Look at your objective to decide which type of content to send and which approach to take. Whether the objective is branding, selling something, reminding consumers of an event or a promotion, or just providing information, the medium needs to be tailored.

Step 3. Send the multimedia content.

You will have the best success with the following:

- **Videos:** Under 30 seconds; keep them fun and engaging.

- **Audios:** Under 60 seconds; keep them fun, engaging, and informational.

- **Images:** For special offers that are time-sensitive.

Step 4. Repeat.

I recommend you send one SMS or MMS message weekly to stay in touch.

Mobile Ads

Not only can you target people who are searching around the Web on their computers, but you can also run ads that target people who are using a mobile phone. What this allows you to do is understand their mentality, but also cater the entire web site experience driving them to mobile responsive sites or mobile optimized landing pages.

To Do: How to Start Generating Revenue with Mobile Ads

To get started with generating revenue with mobile ads, follow these steps:

Step 1. If you do not already have an account on Google AdWords, go to www.adwords.google.com and set one up.

Google still maintains the vast majority of the market share. But here are four other popular places that accept mobile ads:

- Yahoo!

- Facebook

- YouTube
- Twitter

Step 2.   When creating the campaign on the particular advertiser, make sure you select Create a Mobile Ad.

There is a different set of options on the advertiser sites that are strictly devoted to mobile.

Step 3.   Select the keywords you are going to target.

In this case, less is more, but you need enough to test. Here are some free keyword-selector tools:

- www.Wordtracker.com
- www.google.com/sktool

Step 4.   Craft the ad, keeping in mind several guidelines:

- Mobile text ads contain two lines of text with a limit of 12 or 18 characters per line, depending on the language in which you write your ad.
- With this limitation on space, every word needs to be carefully chosen.
- Remember to include the keywords you have purchased in your ad.
- Include a clear call to action.
- The web site you are sending the traffic to shows up on the third line, if you want to enter one.

Step 5.   If applicable (100% recommended), select the option that allows customers to connect directly to your business phone.

This will put a call link next to the web site.

Step 6.   Drive traffic to a mobile-friendly/mobile responsive page.

Step 7.   Split test with different pages and ads; generate various statistics and analytics.

Step 8.   Monitor your traffic and your conversions daily, if not two to three times a day.

Google has a great ad-performance report system, allowing you to track everything you could possibly need. In fact, Google information is so powerful and all-inclusive, you could spend your entire day just looking at the reports (not recommended). You can track things like visitor sources, visitor locations, time on your site, and what pages they viewed. You can even do a site overlay that allows you to see exactly the places your visitors are clicking. In terms of reporting, you can run reports to see whether you are meeting your goals and conversions, as well as general reports to give you a macro-level view of your traffic.

Step 9. Test, optimize, and repeat.

As with traditional pay-per-click, you are going to find that there are certain phrases that pull and provide a much better ROI than others. Integrate the words and ads that perform the best and dump those that do not.

Step 10. Move on to another advertising site.

You should master one ad site before jumping to Facebook, YouTube, and the others. There are hundreds of places where you can place mobile ads. You will, however, find that steps 2 and 3 will produce the bulk of your ROI (the old 80/20 rule).

Step 11. You can also sponsor ads on various free games and applications available on smartphones. Depending on your target demographic, this can prove to be another interesting source of eyes.

Voice Broadcasts

A *voice broadcast* is simply that: a short recorded message that gets blasted out to hundreds or thousands of people. Typical uses for voice broadcasts are promoting major events or campaigning. Ever get those recorded campaign calls? That's a voice broadcast. Voice broadcasts apply to regular phones as well as mobile phones. Your objective is to use voice broadcasts only when you have good information to convey. Do not use the broadcast just for the sake of using it. Make sure that people are not on the do-not-call lists as well.

Here are some fun uses for voice broadcasts:

- **Final reminders**, such as attending an event or coming on a webinar
- Special offers
- Product promotions
- Just to say hi

To Do: How to Get Started with Voice Broadcasts

To get started with voice broadcasts, follow these steps:

Step 1. Sign up for a phone-dialer solution.

Here are our recommendations:

- www.ringcentral.com
- www.voiceshot.com
- www.voicebroadcasting.com
- www.callfire.com
- www.simplycast.com

Step 2. Load your phone numbers into the system.

Make sure that you are adhering to state laws because there are various do-not-call rules and regulations.

Step 3. Create the audio message adhering to these guidelines:

- Make sure you sound upbeat and relaxed.
- Clear and concise information will outperform the rest.
- Keep the length to less than 30 seconds.

Step 4. Let the dialer run its course.

Most of these systems can dial 1,000 phone calls simultaneously or up to 1,000,000 per day. Yeah, it's pretty crazy.

Voice broadcasts are just that simple. We have used this for our events and have seen the attendance rate climb as much as 20%. We also have associates who have used voice broadcasts as an eleventh-hour effort for an event that was about to flop, and their attendance rate literally tripled! It is simply another means of getting your message across. Because most people have their mobile phones attached to their hips, we prefer to send voice broadcasts only to mobile phones rather than typical house lines. Our listening rate is much higher, and there are fewer people on do-not-call lists for mobile phones.

Mobile is growing faster than any other online marketing method, tactic, or technique. I've given you the tools to implement; it's now your turn to pick and choose which ones will make the most sense for your business and get them into action. Start by collecting mobile numbers. Then test the waters with a basic SMS campaign. Get a bit more daring with MMS messaging, and then move over to some mobile ads. You could put yourself years ahead of your competition and get the lion's share of the revenue from this great marketing source.

6

Virtual Reality Worlds: The Hows and Whys of This Unique Marketing Universe

Marketing using virtual reality worlds is the one tactic that is tough for many to grasp. One of the promises that I made in the beginning of the book was to give you tactics that you could jump on before anyone else. This chapter discusses one of those tactics, the virtual reality world.

Although three-dimensional (3-D) worlds have been around for over 10 years, they still have not become mainstream. With some of the recent inventions hitting the marketplace (Google Glass as an example), I firmly believe that virtual universes will gain in popularity. At the time of writing this chapter, Facebook had just purchased a virtual reality company, Oculus Rift, for $2 billion dollars. It seems Facebook wants to build the largest virtual reality world social network.

Because this is a book focused on digital marketing, I do not get into the uses of virtual reality in an offline environment (this will come in a future book), but the possibilities with offline are endless as well. With that said, these environments take a very large time commitment and expense. As always, I will give you different options and tactics to do things on the cheap. When put into place, these 3-D worlds can prove to be your most effective lead generator, sale closer, and cost saver.

Let me take a step back now that I have your eyes curious and your full attention. Virtual reality worlds are just that. They are 3-D, Web-based communities that allow interaction among users and devices by way of the Internet.

In general, virtual reality has a variety of uses. The whole intent of virtual reality is to convince you and your mind that you're actually there, alive in this make-believe world. It brings the experience and interaction to life, even though you are behind a computer or another device and not there in person. The lines of "real life" get blurred very quickly.

Picture this:

- 3-D people walking around, interacting and talking. They don't really exist, but they represent people who do in some way.

- Communication using webcams, headsets, microphones, and text chat.

- People from all walks of life and from around the world who might never have met otherwise.

- The ability to walk around, drive cars, purchase goods and services, and do pretty much *anything* you would do in your actual life.

- A world that seems so real, you start thinking it *is* real.

Sometimes your mind continues to believe that this can't be real, it isn't real, and it's fake. It will take some conditioning of your mind (after you start engaging in these virtual worlds) to understand the concept.

Here are some of the common myths about virtual reality worlds:

84%.

- **Everyone is fake or acts fake**. Eighty-four percent of people reported that when they join the various virtual worlds, they create people—avatars—that represent themselves. Yes, that does leave 16 percent of avatars *16%.* who are not entirely representative of their true selves. Typically these people make minor adjustments, rather than entire modifications of their real personas.

- **It's nowhere near real life**. Many times this is more like real life than your own real life. People host parties and business events. Attend training. Interview for jobs. Shop. Practice foreign languages. Work in global teams. All virtually.

- **It's only for kids**. The average age across most virtual *30* reality worlds is just over 30.

- **The only thing to do in these communities is play games**. Yes, you can play games, but this is only a small fraction of what's done in these worlds.

Here are the key driving factors to the rise in virtual reality usage:

- The technology continues to improve drastically, both the web sites that house some of the virtual reality worlds as well as wearable devices that enhance the experience.

- The death of real-world retail. Most people go to traditional retail stores so they can experience a product (or service). If you can emulate that experience from the comfort of your own home and save money, why wouldn't you want to give it a try?

- We love to be educated. I just walked through an exhibit on Japanese beetles and learned more about beetles in five minutes than I could have learned after reading three books on the subject.

- Mobile continues to (and will continue to) climb, allowing you to enter these worlds instantly from any device anywhere on the planet.

- We are always looking for new and amazing experiences. Want to experience bungee jumping without leaving the house? It can be done.

- Both consumers and businesses have less discretionary income and much smaller travel budgets. They use tools like Gotomeeting.com more than ever but always look for ways to make the interaction more lifelike.

Check out these examples of some of the different things you can do in a virtual environment:

- Instead of attending that rock concert you wanted to go to, check out the same show in a virtual world. Grab some drinks and snacks, and gather around the computer (the bigger the monitor, the better). You will be able to view the avatars performing live, or in some cases live streaming video from the band's studio.

- Think you need to visit the doctor for a diagnosis? Guess again! Go to the doctor's office online, turn on your webcam, and you're in business. Need some tests run? Your doctor can order a nurse to your house or send you at-home testing supplies!

- Want to interact with the Mayo clinic but you live thousands of miles away? Check out its presence in www.SecondLife.com and attend one of the upcoming lectures.

- Want to fly in your employees for a yearly sales meeting, but don't want to spend the money? Host the same meeting on a site like www.SecondLife.com.

- Need to purchase a new camera? Visit the camera store in one of the various virtual worlds, interact with a salesperson, purchase the product, and have the real thing shipped to your home or office.

- Looking for sales leads? Visit one of the thousands of networking locations on the various sites. These are typically labeled "networking lounges."

Anything you would want to do in person (yes, everything) can be done over the Web in the comfort of your own home or office.

The Basics of Virtual Reality World Communities

Let's switch gears just a bit here and chat about the different virtual communities you can potentially leverage for your business, along with some additional background information to help you understand the lingo a bit better.

There are various common threads among most virtual worlds:

- Typically they are run by user-generated content and supplemented with businesses that build presences and content.
- Users can purchase and own virtual land.
- Currency can be exchanged and typically needs to be converted.
- There are various e-commerce applications and functionality, so you're able to buy products and services in real time.
- They are regulated to comply with the various real international laws.

Here are some of the virtual-world terms you should be aware of:

- **Avatars:** The term is derived from Sanskrit and relates to a "mental traveler" in Indian fairy tales. In the virtual world, it is the character you use to represent yourself and communicate with others.

- **Community:** The people or residents who inhabit the virtual space.
- **Currency:** Most of the virtual worlds have their own form of currency, which typically can be converted into USD or other forms of real money.
- **Emotes:** These express emotions in a virtual world (laughing, crying, smiling, and so on).
- **Grid:** The technology and platform behind the virtual world.
- **Latency:** The lag of movements in motion. It's measured in the delay of the actual change of position versus the response time. The faster your computer and Internet connection, the lower the latency you will experience.
- **Teleport:** To fly to another location in the virtual space.
- **Universe:** The collection of all entities and the space they are embedded in for a virtual world. Each virtual reality site has its own "universe," so to speak.

There are hundreds of popular virtual communities and worlds with thousands of users in existence that are much less popular. Let's zero in on the most popular ones that you need to be concerned with.

www.SecondLife.com

Let's start with the community that has received the most media attention and is considered the main virtual reality world.

Second Life was launched in June 2003 by Linden Labs. It allows its residents to interact with each other, socialize, conduct business, and so on, across its grid. You must be 18 or older to use Second Life, and between the ages of 13 and

18 to use Teen Second Life. This is an important distinction for marketing purposes to know that users are 18 and older.

From a numbers standpoint, Second Life has amassed 36 million registered users and has 1 million active users each month. The statistic that stands out is from 2003–2013 when there were 3.2 billion U.S. dollars of virtual transactions.

Registration is free for personal use. If you want a premium membership, there are small monthly fees. If you wish to purchase land, there are small monthly fees for that as well depending on how large your space is. A big advantage of purchasing land is that you can start controlling the marketing space. Most of your competitors will not be on these virtual sites. Get your land before they do.

Much as in the other virtual worlds that will be outlined next, currency can be exchanged. In Second Life, the currency used is Linden dollars. The exchange rate from Linden dollars to USD and to other currencies varies based on market factors—buy and sell rates.

There have been live concerts in Second Life, government embassies established, businesses with full-blown, retail-like spaces and education and training going on pretty much 24/7, to name just a few of the applications. They have also started integrating wearable technology in with the platform. With this addition, I see the virtual world taking off much faster than as of late.

www.ActiveWorlds.com

Active Worlds is a little different from the rest. It is a 3-D world platform with a browser that runs on Windows. (Yes, this helps Bill Gates's wallet grow even larger!) Originally, Active Worlds' programmers wanted to integrate a 3-D browser. Think of Firefox or Internet Explorer in 3-D. Instead, it has morphed into another Second Life.

For consumers, they can play around with their avatar in one of the 1,000 different worlds across the platform, interacting with each other, playing games, or purchasing goods and services.

For businesses, this has been a solid platform on which to develop buzz, sell products, support customers, and provide demos and training.

The advantage of www.ActiveWorlds.com over www.SecondLife.com is that the cost to develop a presence is easier and much less expensive. (To develop a full-blown store on www.SecondLife.com, you are looking at upwards of $5,000 to $10,000 or more.) Your time to market on www.ActiveWorlds.com will be much quicker than on www.SecondLife.com. ActiveWorlds is also business-centric. The company understands that virtual-reality-world marketing is growing in popularity and it has catered many offerings and support to businesses while making it effortless for consumers to buy. The company is trying to bring the www.Amazon.com experience to the virtual world!

www.There.com

www.There.com is an online getaway where you can hang out with your friends and meet new ones, all in an abundant 3-D environment. It is among the simpler platforms. It currently boasts around two million members, and it has hosted some pretty recognizable stop-bys from people like Yellowcard, The Beastie Boys, Korn, and MIMS, along with events like races and concerts on its platform.

www.There.com also has a cool tool called ThereIM (nice play on words, huh?). ThereIM allows you to communicate with other ThereIM users, but without the need to be logged in to the www.There.com virtual world. The technology is similar to instant messaging. The advantage is that you can still use your avatar to communicate with people, so it's not simply texting back and forth.

A lot of commerce and business is taking place on this platform, because it's less crowded and a bit easier to use. As the membership continues to increase, the number of islands created and amount of business being done on these islands will increase, as well.

www.Kaneva.com

Kaneva is a platform that is changing and expanding quite a bit. It has millions of users on a regular basis.

Kaneva combines the social-networking aspect and a virtual world with the focus on commerce and entertainment. It's a much more laid-back, fun environment than many of its competitors. What is interesting is that each new member gets a Kaneva City Loft—their own 3-D space. They can tweak their space and furnish it with their own unique style using virtual furniture and accessories.

www.Worlds.com

Having a presence since 1994, www.Worlds.com has been able to grab some significant market share while perfecting its technology. It has proprietary technology along with quite a few strategic partnerships such as Pearson, Time Warner, Hanson, and even the New York Yankees. This allows the company to combine the best of both worlds (no pun intended). It brings excellent graphics, text chat, voice chat, video, and e-commerce to its platform. In the 3-D communities, visitors can interact, visit different worlds, and connect with one another.

www.Worlds.com is similar to www.SecondLife.com. One key difference, however, is that www.Worlds.com really did pioneer the technology and the social networking aspect of 3-D communities well before it started to become mainstream. Its site is easy to navigate, making it a must-adopt virtual world in your marketing activities! To top it off, it is fully committed to charity and outreach throughout the world. For that, the company gets an extra thumbs up!

Moove

The Moove site allows you to create a room, create groups, and chat via instant messaging with a 3-D spin. It's currently a smaller site with about 1.5 million users. Put Moove toward the bottom of your list of sites to leverage, but keep it on your radar. This virtual site would appeal to people targeting a younger audience.

www.IMVU.com

I saved this one for last because it is not a traditional virtual 3-D world. Instead, IMVU is more of an instant-messaging service, forum, and chat room with the 3-D twist. It was founded in 2004 and has since won numerous awards. IMVU is an online destination for people of all ages to meet each other in 3-D. There are plenty of people to meet; they host more than 100 million registered users.

Members of IMVU have fun meeting new people with similar interests and expressing themselves through personalizing their 3-D avatars, digital rooms, music, and home pages. Users also devote time to customizing their individual home pages, setting up public and private rooms, and creating and participating in user groups. These groups are similar to forums and chat rooms.

IMVU also maintains the world's largest digital-goods catalog, with more than ten million items!. The only key difference between IMVU and the more traditional worlds is that you're not flying around a virtual space and visiting different islands and communities. Again, you're using 3-D chat and participating in different groups that have 3-D scenes.

Because this one sets itself apart from the rest, I wanted to provide some specific information geared toward just this virtual world.

To Do: How to Market Using IMVU

To market using IMVU, follow these steps:

Step 1.   Visit www.IMVU.com and sign up for an account.

Step 2.   Choose your avatar and username.

Make your avatar representative of your personality.

Because social marketing is meant to be a bit less formal and is focused on building relationships, it's recommended that you keep your profile personal in nature.

Step 3.   Link your address book to the virtual world (if using Gmail, AOL, Yahoo!, or Hotmail).

Step 4.   Show the real you.

Load up your profile with some personal and business information. Make sure you include a variety of your interests to spark some interesting chats.

Step 5.   Decorate your room.

Your room is basically like your own little space where you can invite others in.

- Get creative with your room, and make it match your unique style. I decked mine out for a fun section, as well as a business area that was more formal.

- Use your credits to purchase fun things to add to your room.

Step 6.   Find people.

This tool is similar to the search functions of social networks like Facebook.

What is amazing about the system is that you can search for people in certain locations, by age, what they are looking for, friends, chatting, networking, and so on.

When you find someone you would like to chat with, view the person's profile and select Invite to Chat. This will transport you both back to your room for some informal chatting.

Step 7. Build out your home page.

Much as with AIM profiles, IMVU builds you out a home page and autopopulates it with some standard information such as name, age, and location.

- Add the rest of the information to make the page complete. I like to write on here exactly what I'm looking for: networking and chatting.

- Keep in mind that it also links to your room, so make sure your room is ready with different furniture and accessories so that you appear to be a bit more advanced than a newbie.

Step 8. Browse the various groups and join in!

This is where the bulk of your business networking will take place (in groups).

Start off by visiting www.imvu.com/groups to see all the different groups, but don't get overwhelmed by the large number (more than 350,000).

Zero in on a group or two where your target market will be hanging around. For example, there is a group called Entrepreneurs. I joined the group and instantly began to contribute.

Groups are similar to web forums and the tactics are similar, as well:

- Contribute some great content. As with the old saying, people don't care how much you know until they know how much you care.

- Reply and post to different threads.

- Find and friend people of interest. You're building your 3-D world!

Step 9. Check out the different live chat rooms, and pick some of interest.

- There are typically around 25,000 live chat rooms at any given time across IMVU.

- Check out the names for topics of interest.

- After you're in the chat, start a conversation and learn about the different people there.

- If you find people of interest, click on their avatar and select Add to Friends List. This is much like "friending" across different social marketing web sites.

On a final note, this can get addicting. In fact, I'm on the site now trying to multitask between work and play. Be selective about whom you talk to and what groups you join. Join groups of which you can be a contributing member; don't just join groups for the sake of joining (or with the idea of just marketing your services or products). Used effectively, this web site (along with the other virtual worlds) can be a major marketing weapon!

Other Worlds

Virtual reality worlds are popping up left and right (with many others going out of business). I recommend doing some general searches for your niche along with the phrase "virtual world" to see if there are any niched virtual reality worlds you should look at.

The big thing to watch out for is the difference between virtual reality world marketing and networking and sites that focus on game playing or role playing. Virtual communities in general will have a playful feel, but steer away from ones that don't encourage doing business.

How to Leverage the Trend

Now that you know the basics of virtual reality worlds and the different virtual spaces that are getting the most play, let's shift our focus to how to leverage this growing trend. First, let's do a mini-recap of what you have learned about the virtual worlds and look at the advantages and disadvantages of jumping on the virtual train.

Advantages include the following:

- No location barriers
- Demonstrate products in real time
- Awesome user experiences with massive interaction
- Ability to get in touch with peoples' emotions
- Ability to capture market share before everyone else does
- Another sales channel
- Can be tied into wearable technology for an even deeper experience

Disadvantages include the following:

- Not every company will benefit from marketing its products and services in these virtual worlds. If you're a very small company and you intend to stay small, this is not a great space to play in. If you're locally targeted in your marketing, this will also pose a challenge. Don't expect millions of people to be on these spaces within 20 minutes of your house or office. (But it doesn't hurt to test it out first though, right? This is cutting-edge technology, and you won't know if it doesn't work until you try!)

- It is expensive to build advanced platforms. (So start with the easier-to-use sites that require little to no cash outlay for startup.)

- Expect longer lead times (one to four months). When everything is executed correctly, you should be able to cut down your lead times.

There are so many ways to leverage virtual reality worlds. Check these out:

- **Hosting meetings/events:** Large virtual gatherings are the fastest-growing trend in the 3-D space. Why is there even a need to fly anywhere anymore?

- **Sales calls with prospects:** Why not have your prospect visit your virtual space and chat in a much less formal, yet interactive setting? The content sticks much more than in a traditional call, and seems much more like an actual meeting, rather than a phone meeting.

- **Branding:** People are flying around these portals, so why not have a virtual storefront to brand your products and services?

- **Product launches:** Many people and businesses have announced product launches over TV, on the radio, and even with a press release. Announce a product release in your virtual world to the masses!

- **Demonstrations of your product or service:** Videos are a great way to show a product demonstration, but a live virtual demo is much more powerful (and two-way). Think about all the products on sites like QVC that have to be demonstrated to show their effectiveness—you could be doing these exact demonstrations in these communities, live.

- **Digital product sales:** E-commerce is a huge part of the virtual worlds across the Net. Many of the visitors are prospects browsing for products and services. You might as well have something ready to sell them!

- **Education/seminars:** Teleseminars and webinars are big business. Let's take these events to a whole different level.

- **Training employees/contractors:** Instead of flying people in from around the world, host employee training in your secure virtual space.

- **Live entertainment:** Bands, artists, musicians; think of the potential!

- **Charity auctions:** Events go over well in the various virtual communities. Try to run an auction to raise money for your favorite charity.

- **Company communication:** Instead of using just plain chat, spice it up with one of the 3-D chats.

Virtual Trade Shows and Events

The trade show industry and the live-event industry in the United States (and the world, for that matter) are very lucrative. The best part is that they appeal to a whole slew of industries, from business, finance, and entrepreneurship to pets, engineering, and food. Think about attending a trade show in general. What are some of the different elements typically in place?

- Booths of varying sizes and shapes
- Sponsors
- Giveaways (everyone loves swag)
- Attendees
- Product/service demonstrations

- Products/services for sale
- Product literature
- Networking
- Entertainment and education

Case Study

CUNA Mutual Group was looking for an alternative to its annual convention. With an uncertain economy, the company saw its attendance numbers drop. It replicated the same feeling of the live conference in a virtual reality world platform and reduced the fee to 0 for attendees.

The Results:

- More than 1,000 attendees
- A more diverse crowd because there was no travel cost
- Substantial cost savings (93 percent) to both CUNA Mutual and the actual attendees
- Overall satisfaction rates over 90 percent

Comparison Between Live and Virtual Trade Shows

Following are some comparisons between live shows (being there in person) and attending a trade show that is 100 percent virtual.

- **Booths of varying sizes and shapes:** This is the easy one because it's the Web. There is plenty of space available, as well as the capability to deck out your booth. In fact, because of the minimal costs, you can do much more than you could afford to do at a physical event.
- **Sponsors:** Most events have sponsors, and virtual trade shows do as well. You can even sponsor the lanyards people wear!

- **Giveaways (everyone loves swag):** Virtual giveaways are easy. Want to give away something tangible? Ask for a snail-mail address and put it in the mail. Send a free report via email. Offer a gift certificate for services and trial samples of your product.

- **Attendees:** What's an event without participants? Visitors can use webcams, text chat, and voice chat, just as if they were there in person!

- **Product/service demonstrations:** Need to show prospects or attendees a product demo? Not a problem. Programmers can make anything happen!

- **Products/services for sale:** We are out to make money, aren't we? You can take credit cards and process orders on the spot!

- **Product literature:** With the click of the mouse, you can send digital files to anyone interested.

- **Networking:** There are plenty of networking lounges in the various virtual trade shows. You can exchange virtual business cards, talk for as long as you'd like, and even drink a glass a beer with a fellow attendee!

- **Entertainment:** Normally, when you're traveling, there are some forms of entertainment. In a virtual space, you may enjoy virtual cocktails along with some music playing in the background.

If you are considering taking trade shows out of your marketing plan, here are some powerful reasons you will probably produce better results by going virtual:

- It's better for the environment.

- There's no physically draining setup and breakdown. You can literally "assemble" your virtual booth in less than an hour, and it can be saved for the next show.

- It's cheaper than sending your entire sales and marketing staff. You might actually be able to cut some full-time sales jobs if those people spend a lot of their time on the road going to these conferences.

Plus, with no travel needed, not only are you doing your part to help the environment, but think of all the time that will be better used than sitting in an airport terminal waiting for the next flight to come in. It's a win-win for everyone.

Advantages of Virtual Trade Shows

Virtual trade shows have quite a few advantages over live, in-person shows.

- **Huge cost savings for both the vendors and the attendees:** This is the main reason more of these keep popping up.
- **Potential for more staff:** It's easier to have people staff a virtual booth than it is to have them staff a real one.
- **Higher likelihood of people keeping product literature:** More often than not, people go back to their hotel rooms and throw out your expensively produced literature. If the documents are virtual, they are much easier and more convenient to store on a hard drive so that it can be easily found when it's needed.
- **Higher attendance:** With the high cost of travel, more people are flocking to virtual trade shows.

Disadvantages of Virtual Trade Shows

Although virtual trade shows have some great advantages over physical trade shows, hosting strictly virtual-only shows has a few disadvantages:

- **Not face-to-face:** Many say "belly-to-belly" is still the best route.

- **Multitasking:** You're hoping people give you their full attention, but chances are they may be multitasking.

- **Technology issue:** For the less technologically inclined, virtual worlds may be tough to pick up quickly.

To Do: How to Have a Successful Booth at a Virtual Trade Show

To create a successful booth at a virtual trade show, follow these steps:

Step 1.   Prepare for this as if you were preparing for a live event.

Do not skimp on this event because it's virtual. Think about the extreme cost-to-spending savings you've got coming your way, and preemptively reinvest some of that into your virtual booth.

Step 2.   Use a mind map to plan out your booth and your strategy.

Set up the booth dimensions, lighting, features, product offers, and all the typical trade show-related items. Before you approach a company to design your booth, know what you want and your expected outcome. When I help plan a trade show, I craft giveaways, contests, and entertainment to drive traffic to the booth. While there, I also make sure that we have ample product and service literature to give away that is tailored to the event.

Step 3.   Find a virtual trade show to attend that will appeal to your target market, and one that is well marketed.

Here are some web sites that list upcoming virtual trade shows that you can attend or exhibit at:

- www.marketplace365.com

- www.eventsinamerica.com

- www.exhiboronline.com

Step 4. Engage a company that specializes in setting up virtual-trade-show booths and one that has a proven track record.

We recommend the following:

- www.expos2.com
- www.inxpo.com
- www.on24.com

Step 5. Drive traffic to your booth.

This should be the easy part! Utilize all the various marketing tactics you are learning to drive as much traffic to your booth as possible:

- Search-engine optimization
- Pay-per-click
- Mobile
- Marketing and cross-promotion in other virtual worlds
- Social media
- Press releases
- Email blasts to your list
- Sponsorship of the event

Step 5.5. Use guerrilla marketing tactics to further attract people to your booth after the event has started. Some ideas include the following:

- Giveaways
- Contests
- Product demonstrations
- Models (yes, eye candy does work even in the virtual world!)

Step 6. Have more than enough staff.

Because this event is virtual, you can make sure that some extra staff members are on hand. Treat this like a physical event. Your staff should be respectful, be dressed accordingly, understand your customers' needs, and be well-versed in any/all product offerings, as well as the intent of the trade show.

Step 7. Have one staff member hanging out in the networking lounge, chatting with others and drumming up business.

Tas Tip

The lounge is the key for people attending conferences, as well. The networking lounges are where a lot of deals are getting inked. Yes, it's great to visit the various vendors at their booths, but a lot of deals are done in a more informal setting. Even virtually.

Step 8. Follow up with the leads quickly.

What's the use of going to a trade show if you're not going to follow up with the leads? This is the biggest mistake people make after attending trade shows. They do not follow up with the leads.

To Do: How to Start Marketing Using Virtual Reality Worlds

To start marketing using virtual reality worlds, follow these steps:

Step 1. Select a site you want to start with.

It's not feasible to develop a presence on all the sites. Start with a smaller site, and then move up to one of the larger ones after you start getting this new world down and become more comfortable in this unique space.

Step 2. Set up your profile/avatar.

Much as with social-marketing profiles and forum profiles, you want to be certain your profiles are all-inclusive and representative of your true self. Yes, you can shave a few years off your age and a few pounds off your weight, but be truthful in the rest! Remember, you are trying to generate business, and a professional, yet personal, profile is a must.

Step 3. Acquire land or space for a storefront if applicable.

This applies to people who are interested in setting up a shop to brand their product or service or to sell it from a virtual storefront. Second Life allows you to purchase land, while some of the others sell buildings and land. This is a sizable investment, so I recommend setting up a shop if you're a business that is doing at least $1 million per year in revenue.

Step 4. Build your presence/storefront.

After you have land or a building, you will most likely need to hire a programmer to help you build out your space. This is where I don't like Second Life and prefer many of the others, like www.IMVU.com. Second Life requires technical expertise to design your storefront and to make it attractive. With IMVU, I get a generic space, but with the push of a button, I can change colors, move around plants, buy products to decorate the space, and make it look more like home. There are pros and cons to both. Making your IMVU space look nice will take little cash; however, with a developer, the job can be done quickly. On the other hand, if you have land and can afford a programmer, the sky is the limit.

Step 5. Network in the various communities.

Treat virtual worlds like real life. Visit groups, chat rooms, and locations you would frequent in real life. Strike up conversations; you will be amazed as to where things can go. Virtual-reality-world marketing is very similar to social marketing; it simply takes things up a few notches because there is a more visual interaction. Make sure you have all the latest and greatest technology to communicate with people.

Step 6. Drive people to your virtual space.

It's one thing to have a virtual space, but it's an entirely different thing to have a virtual storefront that actually produces revenue! Treat your virtual space as if it were another web site that needs traffic to succeed. Use your web marketing tactics to funnel some of your traffic to this space.

Step 7. Use it!

This may sound basic, but there are a surprising number of people who go through all the trouble to establish a virtual presence and then do nothing with it. Review the various ways you can use your virtual space (trade shows, sales meetings, employee training, and so on).

Step 8. Mix things up.

Keep your space fresh and fun. Keep in mind that trends are constantly changing and the technology is becoming more affordable. Staying on top of the latest trends will help your virtual space stand out from the crowd.

Step 9. Constantly track your ROI.

This can become a time-consuming process. Many of our clients have a full-time employee who is 100 percent dedicated to maintaining and networking on their various virtual worlds. Virtual worlds are not for every business. Before you invest a lot of time and energy in this marketing tactic, set up the analytical measurements to make sure you can track your efforts.

Virtual-Reality-World Banner Ads

Traditional banner ads work fine, but people often view them quickly and click on them without looking. People are jumping to a different web site every 34 seconds on average, so most such ads have a negative ROI.

Place some advertisements across a few of the different virtual spaces.

Because only some of the sites allow advertising, and policies differ from one to the next, I will not be giving you a step-by-step how-to list. Instead here are some guidelines:

- Split-test a few different ads. With split testing, you only want to test one element at a time.

- Make sure that the people viewing them are targeted.

- Track and monitor statistics to ensure a solid ROI.

- Commit to no more than a two-month campaign, and set your budget relatively low.

With the rate of people flocking to virtual worlds increasing often largely due to the new wearable technology, there is no reason you should ignore this tactic. It's an awesome way to connect with people on a deeper level without having to bear the crazy travel costs. When you really take a step back and see how this fits nicely into your marketing, it can be a game changer. Virtual-reality-world marketing still has a long way to go before it will be considered mainstream, but that is probably the most exciting part. If this were mainstream, you would already be too late! See you in the virtual world!

7

Video Marketing: Leveraging Video for More Profits

There is no doubt of the huge video craze across the world. This has been fueled with the growth of mobile. Everyone with a mobile device is essentially a journalist. Everything has been shifting from text and audio to video. We want to *see* things rather than just *read* or *hear* them. The social-proof factor ("hey, I saw it instead of just reading it"), entertainment factor, ease of use, and ability to find pretty much anything online continues to drive the video market and its popularity. We want to be able to get things on demand, and fast.

The Video Craze

To further drive the point home that you need to leverage video in your marketing, here are ten different statistics related to marketing with video:

- YouTube.com is the world's second largest search engine.
- Eighty percent of people remember the video ads they saw.

- A third of all online activity is spent watching video.
- Consumers who watch a video about a particular product are 60 percent more likely to buy that product.
- Real estate listings that contain video receive 400 percent more leads.
- Subscriber-to-lead conversion rates increase 51 percent when a video is included in the campaign.
- Nearly everyone who sees a video about a product says the video is helpful in making a buying decision.
- Your web site is 50 times more likely to appear on page one of Google if it contains a video.
- Click-through rates in email increase from two to four times when a video is included.
- Seventy-five percent of executives watch business-related videos at least once a week.

With the ease of the technology at our fingertips, it has become the norm to see videos everywhere. No longer do your prospects and customers just want to read text or view images. They want to be engaged, and engaged through video. They want to see your products or services come to life in video.

The most shocking statistic that I didn't include is this: In 30 days, more video content is uploaded than all three major U.S. networks combined have created in 30 years! In this chapter, I give you everything you need to know to profit from the boom in video and to get a leg up against your competition.

Where Do You Start?

So where do you start? Do you try to create a viral video? Do you create welcome videos for your web site, educational videos for Youtube.com, or do you test the waters with some live video? The answer: It depends on what you have to start with or work with.

Earlier in the book, I asked you to do an audit of your current marketing. What did the audit tell you on the video side? If you are like most business owners, you have very little in the way of video and are most likely starting from scratch. If you are armed with dozens or hundreds of videos, feel free to skip ahead. I have yet to work with many companies that are starting with a substantial amount of videos in their arsenal.

From a video standpoint, here are the most important ones you need to get produced:

- A welcome video on your homepage
- Product- and service-related videos
- Videos for trade shows, conferences, and events that can be played on a television screen or computer
- Videos that can be embedded into your emails
- Testimonials
- Regular educational content for Youtube.com and other video sites
- Videos for search engine optimization purposes

Here is the step-by-step checklist to kick off your video marketing efforts.

To Do: How to Get Started in Online Video

Following are steps for getting started with online video:

Step 1. Decide if you have the team (and talent) to produce the videos in-house or if you need to hire a studio.

This step can get to be a bit complicated. Depending on the shape and size of your business, typically, it makes sense to leverage both a studio and in-house talent. This is also coming from someone who owns a video studio (Guerrilla Video Solutions). Shooting videos each and every month at a professional studio will get to be quite expensive. I recommend getting the "one off" videos produced at a studio, and the monthly educational videos get done in-house. Even though you need to make an investment in equipment, in the long run, it will save you money to do some of the videos in-house.

Step 2.   Write scripts for your one-off videos.

It makes sense to focus on getting your one-off videos produced first and in particular, if you don't have a homepage video, you should start with it. As long as you (or someone on your team) has good presence on camera, it will make sense to have these videos be mainly "talking heads." Your prospects and customers will relate more to seeing faces and body language over anything else.

From a script standpoint, you want to keep the videos short, lively, upbeat and to the point. Keep in mind your prospects and customers care only about themselves. Talk about the benefits you provide and how your product or service will help them. You want to avoid making these videos "me" centric.

I like to have the main points bulleted of my script written out in a bulleted list versus read a full-blown script. I find that when I'm reading word for word, I tend to be boring versus doing the videos ad lib. At the same time, if I don't have the bulleted points, I miss key points.

Step 3.   Hire a studio and get the videos produced.

Armed with your scripts, engage a professional local studio to shoot the videos. They will get you dialed in, coach you during the process, and give you blunt feedback based on your performance. If you want to get the best rate, schedule a half day or full day for the shoot and get as many of the one-off videos produced as possible.

As an aside, I also encourage you to hire a makeup artist to make you (or your talent) even more amazing. Yes I'm encouraging men to get makeup as well. Do you really think your favorite television personalities don't have any makeup on? Come on now.

Have the videos shot on a green screen so you have the ultimate flexibility when editing the videos. The green will allow you to swap in any type of background you can possibly imagine.

From an editing standpoint, rely on the experts, but let them know the focus on the videos and the tone you are after. The more information you can give them about your business and your target market, the better the end result will be.

Step 4. Leverage the videos you get produced.

After you have the final videos in your hand, get them on the Web or in the respective places they should be. From a technical standpoint, use a service such as Wistia.com to host the videos or store them on Amazon S3 and use a plug-in so the videos play quickly. Have you ever watched a video that takes minutes to load? We want the videos to load quickly and not buffer at all. I also want to make sure your videos do not have any ads showing up because you are hosting them with a free service (such as YouTube. com). It looks unprofessional for a video to be loaded on your homepage and for that video to have ads selling products or services for other companies due to the ads.

Step 5. Create your own studio.

In the previous steps, you cranked out the one-off videos to increase the image of your company and give your prospects and customers the ability to better experience your company visually. Congratulate yourself for getting those videos done. Now it's time to turn up the heat and focus on the educational videos that will help fuel leads to your company.

In creating your own studio, you need to find a place at your office (or home office) where you can set things up and ideally leave things. I have found that getting the videos done is not the actual resistance people put up. People put videos on a lower priority due to the time it takes to set up your actual "studio." Find a nice quiet location that you can shoot videos at each month.

Next, move onto spending some money on equipment. There are numerous directions you can take here depending on your budget and the staff you have. I recommend starting with less expensive stuff and working your way up.

You will need:

- A camera
- A stand or tripod for the camera
- A wireless microphone
- A background to shoot on
- A light kit

Rather than give you product-specific information, check out Amazon.com and sort by ratings, or call the experts at B&H, bhphotovideo.com. You will want to get an HD camera and a good microphone. Often, I tell people to spend more money on the microphone than the camera as sound quality is paramount. From a background standpoint, I recommend buying a green screen kit so you can replicate the green screen environment.

You can easily get everything you need for well under a $1,000.

Step 6. Brainstorm the topics for the videos.

These videos are meant to be short and sweet, educational videos. They are going to get leveraged on your blog, on Youtube.com, and other video sites.

I always encourage you to start with the top questions you get asked on a regular basis from your prospects and shoot those first. For example: Hi, this is Michael from Guerrilla Video Solutions. One of the top questions we get asked is, "Isn't video expensive to get produced?"

Keep the videos under three minutes in length.

After you have shot videos on all the top topics, leverage the Google keyword tool and type in random phrases and see what people are searching for.

If you spend several hours writing down video topics you can easily come up with enough videos to shoot for 3–6 months or more.

Remember, keep the content educational versus sales pitchy. If you have a "dry" business that doesn't lend itself to producing fun videos, expand out a bit by talking about things to do in the area and about current events or trends. The objective is to keep shooting videos on a regular basis.

Step 7. Shoot the videos.

Armed with your topics and some bullet points for each video, get to work and shoot the videos. I recommend that you do these in one siting and just crank them out versus trying to do a few a week. I'll try and be optimistic here, but more often than not, these videos do not get done, life gets in the way. Crank them out in an afternoon and schedule the next time for the following month. Once you get good, you can shoot 15–20 videos in about 90 minutes.

Step 8. Edit the video, as needed.

I prefer to do very light editing, if any at all. Rougher-cut videos are better perceived by prospects and do a better job of creating relationships with your viewers. If you have someone on your team who can do this, leverage a program such as Imovie or Final Cut Pro, or you can outsource this piece to your local studio or a freelancer on a site such as elance.com.

You should include the following:

- An introduction
- Outro (end the videos in a similar way with a call to action)
- A unique landing page link at the bottom of the video
- Music
- Good lighting and sound

Be careful here, as you can spend considerable money in the editing phase. I've always been for doing it yourself, but it depends on your team and resources.

Step 9. Deploy the videos.

After you have the videos edited and your calls to action ready, deploy the videos across the Web. The #1 site for video is still (and most likely will always be) YouTube.com.

When posting the videos, make sure to optimize them correctly (very similar to a blog post). You should have a compelling title with keywords, a compelling description with keywords, and various tags associated with the video.

You can also publish the video on other video sites such as DailyMotion.com, Vimeo.com, and MetaCafe.com.

A tool such as TrafficGeyser.com or TubeMogul.com can be used to help automate the process of posting to a lot of sites quickly.

Step 10. Create your next batch.

The most important piece to successfully generate more traffic with videos is to stay consistent in the number of videos you produce. Even if you are not able to do 10–20 videos a month aim for 5, but do them consistently month after month. Leverage the Google keyword tool to continually find new topics to shoot.

Video Search Engine Optimization

Let's face it, Google loves video for many reasons. One reason (from a profit standpoint) is the simple fact that Google owns Youtube.com. It is in Google's best interest for YouTube.com to succeed. A great tactic to add to your arsenal is video search engine optimization. This is the practice of getting videos ranked on page one of Google versus focusing solely on your web site. If you read the statistics at the beginning of this chapter, you should again realize that video produces better marketing results.

The beauty of video search engine optimization combined with regular search engine optimization is it gives you the ability to control multiple page one rankings. Compare the page one of Google to prime real estate. Everyone wants a piece. If you have both your web site on page one in addition to a video, you control 20 percent versus the 10 percent you had before.

To Do: How to Take Your Videos to Page One of Google

Here is a step-by-step list to execute video search engine optimization with deadly precision:

Step 1. Pick the video you want to get ranked on page one.

This part takes a bit of strategic thinking. You are aiming for a video that is strong and that has a solid call to action. In a perfect world, you are able to shoot some videos in a professional studio in addition to ones in your home made studio. The educational videos you are shooting will work well, but again, make sure there is a call to action.

Step 2.   Transcribe the video.

After you have selected the video, transcribe it word for word (eliminating any "Ums" of course).

Step 3.   Select the keyword(s) you are aiming to rank for.

Use tools such as Wordtracker.com or the Google Keyword Planner to locate good keywords. The ones that work well for video search engine optimization tend to have low to medium competition and are typically 3–5 words. They also work best when they are location-specific. For example, Phoenix pool cleaning.

Step 4.   Load the video onto YouTube.com, paying close attention to optimization.

This step is the most critical. When you load in the video you selected, make sure to correctly optimize the video. This means loading in a keyword-rich title tag, a keyword-rich description, keywords, and proper tags. You should also load in the transcription you did in Step 2, modifying it slightly to include the keywords you are aiming to get the video ranked for. Once this is complete, take the video live.

Step 5.   Draft a press release about the video.

To be deemed newsworthy, there must be some type of news announcement versus just saying "a new video was published." Your angle could be something along the lines of, "Local Phoenix pool company has discovered a new way to clean your pool in 5 minutes or less." In this press release, the secret sauce is the links. You want to include 1–3 links back to your Youtube.com video link using the keywords you are going after. So, for example, if you are targeting Phoenix pool cleaning, include that phrase in your press release with a link to your YouTube.com video. What this is doing is creating a variety of quality backlinks to your YouTube.com video.

Step 6. Submit the press release for distribution.

After you have the press release drafted and optimized, submit it for distribution.

Step 7. Build additional links to the video.

After the press release goes out, chances are your video can wind up on page one of Google within the week. To further help your chances, build some additional quality links to the video. You can link to the video from social media, on your blog, on your podcast, or on other article and news sites. The more quality links you have, the better.

Tas Tip

This tactic alone can get you massive traffic. Having double search-engine rankings will drastically increase your natural, organic search-engine traffic.

Make sure you are tracking your video results. For example, if you have a cooking video on how to cook the perfect turkey, include a link in the video to a specific landing page that you set up like this: *yourdomain*.com/turkey. You can then check the traffic of that specific page to see whether the video generated any traffic, opt-ins, or sales.

Taking a Video Viral?

When it comes to video, time and time again, the #1 question I get asked is, "How can I make my video go viral?" The answer: very rarely by accident. For whatever reason, marketers and business owners alike, love the term "viral video." The challenge is that when asked to throw some different viral video examples, rarely are any of them business-related. They are things like the free hugs campaign, the double rainbow, twerking, pranks, and beyond. Around the time of "the big game," people tend to remember the commercials, but those often fade and they remember the others. One of the big mistakes marketers tend to believe is that any publicity is good publicity, but you can't get any farther from the truth. You want to obtain publicity that shows your company or your brand in the highest regard possible.

Please don't get me wrong, having a video go viral can be a good thing, but you want to make sure the video portrays your company in the right light.

Here are three things to have in your back pocket should you want to embark on the viral video journey:

- Craft a video that brings people to extreme emotions. At the time of writing, a new video surfaced from TD Canada. In the video, TD Canada transformed its ATM into an automated thanking machine, and it gave amazing gifts to unsuspecting customers. It already has 1,000,000 views, and it's only been five days. It reflects the type of emotional response you are going after. If the video isn't amazing, it will not stand a chance at going viral.

- Put some ad dollars behind the video. You can start with YouTube.com ads, throw $1,000 or so at the campaign to drive a few thousand targeted visits, and grow it from there. Most viral videos have had huge ad budgets. If you have some additional money to invest, pay a high-end news site to write a story or feature the video.

- Spread the video everywhere you can. Spreading is what takes a video viral. If the video is worth spreading and you get it in front of enough people, things can take off organically.

Shifting from YouTube to Ustream, Livestream, and Google Hangouts

There is no question that YouTube.com is a powerhouse of a site. At the time of writing, it boasts over 1 billion users. I encourage you to continue marketing with YouTube.com, but I also want you to understand the limitations. Like traditional TV, it is a one-way conversation.

Imagine being able to interact with a reality TV show in real time, or get live feedback on something you are considering purchasing? Live streaming video and live web-based experiences can help take your marketing to an entirely different level. Rather than simply view other peoples' content, get in action producing high quality content that will drive more leads, more sales and more profits to your business.

Tas Tip

It's all about the user interaction and user experience. This goes for everything, including user-generated content, webinars, video, virtual worlds, mobile marketing, social media, and beyond. The key take-away with these concepts is to make sure that the users can get involved and ask questions in real time. How fun is it to sit and watch? Depending on what it is, it can be fun. Want to make it more fun and turn it into an experience? Get the users involved.

Two Options for Viewing Video

There are only two options for viewing or watching video online:

- **Option 1:** You can watch a video presentation on how to prepare a high quality organic meal on YouTube.

- **Option 2:** You can view a stream-broadcasting at 7:30 PM at my house in my kitchen as I prepare the dish live taking questions and providing feedback, live.

Which option do you prefer? Option 1 is great for busy people who can't make the time, but most will go with Option 2 so that they can be a part of the event. To facilitate the interaction, I can allow for questions as I move forward in the process and ask if others have any tips for me to improve the dish I'm making. To further expand the reach, I would have someone manage my social media platforms and provide live updates during the process. People can even watch live right from Facebook. If the audience had a webcam plugged in, I could even turn the camera to them, allowing them to demonstrate something.

Advantages of live video:

- Involves user interaction
- Typically brings higher attendance
- Allows viewers to share the thrill
- Appeals to the different senses and emotions
- Can be leveraged as static video in the future

Disadvantages of live video:

- Can bring up scheduling issues. Not everyone is able to make a live presentation, with many people expecting a recording.
- It involves some lag time, meaning that quicker computers and Internet connections are preferred.

As we have done with the other disadvantages, we can provide a rebuttal. If people can't attend your live stream, they can still replay it. The advantage of this over YouTube is you still get some of the live experience on your computer.

In regard to having faster computers and Internet speeds, this used to be the case for most feeds. There was always a delay and some lag time. This situation has improved greatly and will continue to get better as computer speeds, Internet connections, and the actual streaming-video technology improve.

Which factors cause the live-video trend to increase?

- Being able to experience things has become the latest trend and now really the norm.

- People are continuing to flock to the Web for video, whereas traditional TV viewing continues to decline. YouTube, for example, reaches more U.S. adults ages 18–34 than any other cable network.

- People love to be entertained and don't want to miss out.

- Everyone can easily start to stream their own show from a mobile device or tablet with ease.

- The technology and quality have improved drastically over the last few years.

Let's talk about mobile for a bit. You read the mobile chapter and understand that it's the fastest-growing trend talked about in this book. Take it a step further. You can stream video live from your iPhone, iPad, Droid, or other device directly to Ustream.TV. Think of the power here. You can report on the latest news and stream video from anywhere in the world with the push of a button! You don't need any fancy video equipment, a makeup artist, a sound guy, or a lighting crew; you simply need your mobile phone.

Tas Tip

I've been using the word *trend* a lot in this book. Note the difference between a trend and a fad. Trends are backed by statistics; fads are things that come and go. Don't be like Blockbuster and miss a critical trend that drives you out of business.

There are limitless ideas for using live streaming video in your marketing and branding. Check out these ideas, hot off the press:

- **Conferences:** Virtual worlds are great, but they assume you will be hosting the event solely in a virtual world. Let's take an example. You are a motivational speaker, hosting one of your semiannual events on how to get yourself motivated in a down economy. A real "upper" topic, huh? The last two words, *down economy*, are going to deter a lot of people from flying in and attending your event. Rather than missing out on all that business, stream the feed live for a fraction of the cost of a live event. Your attendance rate will skyrocket, and you're not limiting yourself solely to people who will physically attend.

- **Product/service launches:** What better way to tell the world about a new product or service offering than by announcing it live to your listeners, and taking orders on the spot (think of the Home Shopping Network on the Web).

- **Concerts:** Stream your concert for free or for a small price for raving fans who want to watch you but can't attend.

- **Parties:** Just reached a business milestone and want to celebrate with your staff? Get on Ustream, toast each other, and drink some bubbly!

- **Interviews:** Interviews are a great way to interact. Ustream was used widely in the recent election by both candidates.

- **Education:** Most people on Ustream use the service to educate their viewers on different topics of interest and combine chat with Q&A in the process.

- **Charity:** Various events and stunts have been hosted on Ustream (and others) to raise money for charity, from sleeping strikes, to playing the guitar for tips, and even all the way to playing video games for 50-plus hours.

- **Chatting/Q&A session:** Looking for the ultimate interaction? Host a chat session with your viewers, taking questions live on the spot! Take it up a level by allowing the person asking the question to be seen on his or her webcam. This is where I recommend you focus the bulk of your attention because it's the tactic that produces the most high-quality interaction.

Case Study

Arizona State University has been adopting live video for quite some time. It has used it to better engage with students from a distance learning standpoint, broadcast many events, and get social engagement flowing. The ASU Live TV channel on Ustream.tv has been viewed over 600,000 times. Twitter is integrated into the channel and is getting comments on a regular basis.

One of the biggest objectives was to reach people all over the globe. To date, it has engaged people from over 70 countries throughout the world!

The Key Takeaway: You can reach pretty much anyone, anywhere in the world on any device in real time, allowing people to be part of the experience.

Take note of these live streaming video sites:

- www.Ustream.TV
- www.Justin.tv
- www.Livestream.com
- www.Bambuser.com

Keep in mind, these tactics and steps apply across the board to the others with slight variations. I have zeroed in on Ustream.TV. I recommend that you start off by leveraging Ustream.TV because it's the easiest to use and gain traction with.

To Do: How to Market Using Ustream

To get started with Ustream, follow these steps:

Step 1. Go to Ustream.TV and set up an account.

- Use your brand as the name of the channel or use something creative to stand out from the crowd.

- Invite friends via your email client and social media platforms.

Step 2. Purchase the needed video equipment, or stream right from your mobile device.

Depending on how serious you want to get about live streaming video, you can leverage a good webcam, or you can get an expensive camera and cables and the like. I always recommend starting with the less expensive option first (webcam), and working your way up to a more expensive option.

Step 3. Connect your webcam or video camera to your computer, or boot up your mobile device.

Step 4. Create a show.

- Type the name of the show—for example, Organic Cooking With Sara Smith.

- Upload a logo (use your logo, or have one created).

- Select the best category that fits with what your show is about.

- Add some tags. These are keywords people might be searching for and words/phrases that relate to your topic—for example, organic, organic cooking, healthy living.

- Write a description. You must make this compelling or people won't watch the show. Think of your description as something you would read to decide whether to watch a movie or a show.

Step 5.   Save the show for later.

You don't want to broadcast just yet!

Step 6.   Market the show so you get some attendees.

- Announce it in your other social sites and use other marketing tactics I've trained you on. Sending an email broadcast to your database also works really well.

- Emphasize the fact that it's live video with interaction.

- Post it on the various free sites that allow event postings.

Step 7.   Deliver a solid performance.

- Give away great content.

- Keep it interactive.

- Take questions and feedback.

- The show is prerecorded, so I like to take questions ahead of time and play them as if they were live.

Step 8.   Have a call to action.

What do you want people to do when they come on your show? If your shows are totally informational, that is what your viewers will expect. And, without a call to further action, your interaction with your viewers could end with the conclusion of your program. That would be a waste of all that effort you just put into the program. So, have a mini pitch or call to action at the end of each show. Here are some ideas:

- Ask viewers to sign up for an additional course with you.

- Offer a reduced price on a training product, if they buy within a certain number of hours or days.

- Invite them to sign up for a member site.

- Offer coaching services.

Whatever your business is, you can gear your pitch accordingly. Just don't get into the habit of constantly providing free information without asking for anything in return.

Step 9.   Use the recording after the live show is over.

- Post it on Ustream.TV along with the other video sites (breaking it out into multiple pieces first).

- Give out the recording to your mailing list and other places.

- Even use it on a membership-based web site where people are paying you revenue each month for unlimited access.

Step 10.   Utilize stats and analytics.

Check out your stats right in the dashboard area, and then cross-check that with analytics to make sure you're generating some traffic. This allows you to view statistics from two places.

Internet TV

If you got excited when I talked about live streaming video, you're going to love the next tactic even more: hosting your own live Internet TV channel.

Starting Your Own Internet TV Channel

So you've grasped the concept of live streaming video and fully understand the advantages of live versus static videos (like the ones you browse on YouTube). Now, how about having your own, live TV channel that is broadcasting constantly on the Internet?

When most people think of Internet TV, they think of watching their favorite TV shows or various movies. This has been around on the Net for a few years, and the quality continues to get better with the expansion of high definition (HD). Your very own Internet TV channel has a similar general concept. The difference is you're not a huge TV station, and you're not broadcasting movies or soaps. Instead, your channel is going to be educational in nature and will turn into a lead-generating powerhouse.

To further simplify things, think of this example: One of my favorite networks is ABC. If I were to stay up for 24 hours straight, I would see a mix of things:

- Prerecorded shows
- Commercials
- Live shows, like the news

Your Internet TV channel will be similar in that broad view. You are going to offer some prerecorded materials, host some live events, and stock the waves with commercials and sponsors.

Take a look at some of the reasons you would want to have your own Internet TV station:

- Your own Internet TV station positions you as an expert.
- It gives you a great tool to educate your marketplace.
- It's a medium for you to interview people.
- It gives you another sales channel.
- It generates leads.
- You can earn ad revenue through it.
- It gives you the opportunity to have a constant presence in your space, with the freshest, most up-to-date content available.

Many people have grabbed domains ending in .tv. Not surprisingly, .tv is the assumed natural extension for television, and because of this, .tv domains have great marketing appeal.

To Do: How to Start Your Internet TV Channel

To get started with Internet TV Channel, follow these steps:

Step 1. Develop your station mind map so you know where you're headed.

- What do you want to get out of your television station?
- What content do you want to provide?
- What will be your hours of operation?
- When will you be live versus prerecorded?
- Create a schedule of events and topics.

Step 2. Get a domain.

I recommend getting a domain name just for this endeavor. The .tv domain names have been the most popular for anything related to a television station. What you need to keep in mind is that .tv does not stand for television. It is actually the extension for Tuvalu, the Polynesian island nation.

Step 3. Hire a good team to design and code a web site.

- It should look like a typical web site. The difference: In the middle of the screen, there should be a large television that is streaming your video or broadcasting live.
- Publicize your sponsors.
- Have different sections on your web site where people can browse your products and services, learn more about you, contact you, and carry out all the other typical options.
- Change your site often to reflect current promotions and features.

Step 4. Set up a dedicated area for filming.

Since you will be doing both prerecorded and live videos, you should have an area in your home office (or an off-site office) that is decked out with all the necessary equipment and will look great on film.

Step 5. Purchase suitable equipment for recording video and broadcasting live.

You can get all of this for under $1,000 (re-read the previous video equipment section).

- An HD camera is recommended.
- Audio equipment: microphone, headset, clipped microphone, or even some wireless audio equipment.
- Lighting: Invest in some great lights.
- Green screens. (These are great because they allow for easier editing of video and still photos.)
- Teleprompter, if you want to read from a script.
- Connect your camera to your computer, and get ready to stream live!

Step 6. Get a good web site host that can handle the bandwidth and the constant streaming of video.

Step 7. Record content you can load onto the station.

Don't think you need hundreds of hours of content to launch your station. You can start with just a few hours of content. Reread the ideas for the live events in the earlier part of the chapter for content ideas and things you can do live or prerecord.

Here are some other content ideas:

- Webcam broadcasting 24/7 (or in certain hours)
- Other people's content you can use (with permission)
- Old video recordings
- Testimonials from clients and customers

Step 8. Keep in mind you don't need to have content up 24/7.

- We have four hours of prerecorded content daily, two hours of live stuff, and some commercials mixed in.
- We let that content repeat for six hours.
- We then have 12 hours where there is nothing more than a Microsoft PowerPoint presentation and some music.

The reason we have done this is that we have found the times when people were browsing the station. There is no reason to put up content if very few people are on your web site at a given time! If your audience is largely global, and in different time zones, you will want to consider having a larger amount of content at different times.

Step 9. Host some live events.

Live events are a great draw, as we talked about previously. The difference is you will be hosting your events on your web site rather than appearing on someone else's.

Step 10. Promote your hot new TV channel everywhere.

And when I say everywhere, I mean everywhere.

- Link it on your web sites, social sites, and beyond.
- Send out multiple press releases using a service like www.PRWeb.com.
- Partner with some other people in exchange for free advertising.

Step 11. Step it up a notch!

As your station becomes more popular, you can start commanding various features and money-making opportunities:

- Paid advertising.
- Banner ads on your site.
- High-profile guest interviews. Heck, maybe you will become the next Oprah!

Much as in virtual reality worlds, having your very own Internet TV channel may seem a bit far-fetched, but why not give it a try? Load up a few hours of content, let it rotate, and stream at various times and see what feedback you get. You hold a great advantage if you can also say, "Hi, I'm Mr. Smith. I'm an entrepreneur. By the way, did I mention I have my own Internet TV station?" People gravitate toward experts, and this is another mode to increase your expert status and sell some products and services at the same time. And quite frankly, when you start getting the hang of it, it's rather fun!

The Easy Video Recorder

Now that I have you all worked up to be shooting lots and lots of video, I'm going to make your life ten times easier and talk about my favorite video-shooting device.

Let me set the stage. This device:

- Fits in your pocket
- Shoots HD
- Is easy to use
- Can publish to the cloud instantly or stream live
- Is used by you hundreds of times a day
- Costs less than $200

Drum roll, please... The device is *your mobile phone!*

The video quality on a mobile phone continues to improve with each and every phone that comes out. What's even better is that you already have this device on you wherever you go, so you can easily record "in-the-moment videos." Here are some video examples:

- Record testimonials
- Create video blog posts

- Produce educational videos
- Promote products
- Capture crazy events when you're out and about

My intention is to make your life easier, not more complicated. Using your mobile device versus a full-blown video studio setup will make that happen.

A Show on Real Television?

My claim to fame is being a trend spotter. I'm very good at spotting trends months or years ahead of everyone else and training my students and clients on how to capitalize on these trends.

Internet and live streaming television is here to stay. As we continue to become more and more mobile, we continue to watch these shows from our mobile devices. With that said, I do not see the death of physical television coming anytime soon. Are cable and satellite television going to decline? Of course.

There is a little device that is in millions of households that continues to pick up tracking. This device is called Roku. Do you have one? Roku allows you to search for shows and movies across dozens of different channels to find what you are looking for.

What if you had your own channel that your prospects or customers could watch on their televisions from their Roku devices?

It is as simple as becoming a developer on Roku and making it happen. Because this is a bit techie, I won't go into all of the technical details of making it happen, and simply say it is easier than you think.

If you have enough content to get your Internet TV show going, you can leverage that exact same content on the Roku device, thus reaching an even wider audience.

Take note of this trend and jump on the bandwagon early!

The sky is the limit when it comes to video both static and live, and no longer has it become a nicety to have, but rather a must have. Improve your video, and your profits will improve with it.

8

Leveraging Tools to Speed Up and Automate Your Marketing

As I have said many times, speed is a great advantage when it comes to marketing. Having said that, I understand there are only so many hours in the day to make things happen and that you are most likely resource-constrained. Following is a list of resources broken down by section that you can leverage to improve your marketing and help to automate your marketing. Rather than provide you 50 different options under each, I have limited the options to those I have used personally and capped the total to four options. I want you to see this book as a guidebook or action guide that enables you to move into action rather than stay in analysis paralysis.

Customer Relationship Management

Having a customer relationship management (CRM) tool is the foundation of successful marketing. This tool serves as the hub of all of your contact with your prospects and customers. It also allows you to set up triggers and automation to aid in the process. For example, when a prospect comes in the door, automated emails (or physical direct mail pieces) can get triggered instantly. Those messages would be tracked for open rates, and then some additional triggers could happen based on how that prospect chooses to (or not) interact with those messages. When set up correctly, your CRM tool is instrumental to your business and keeps you and your marketing on track, producing the results you are going after. This tool should be constantly updated for optimum performance. As your business evolves, it should evolve with it.

Tools I recommend are:

- **Salesforce.com:** Largely considered the top CRM tool on the planet, Salesforce.com is definitely worth taking a look at. Although it is overkill for most small businesses, it allows you to grow into a platform versus the other way around.

- **Infusionsoft.com:** This is the tool that I use on a regular basis due to the automation features and heavy email marketing capabilities. Infusionsoft is a CRM tool, an email marketing tool, an affiliate module, and an e-commerce tool all in one.

- **Insightly.com:** If you want something that is easy to use, this is your tool. You can be up and running in minutes and you can put this tool into action.

- **Netsuite.com:** If you are a larger business and want an over-the-top solution, Netsuite.com should be considered. This is not a tool for small businesses. Netsuite.com packs a lot of punch and quite a bit of integration, allowing you to run the bulk of your business with its platform.

I'm a huge fan of salesforce.com and believe that most businesses should start here. Here is a to do list to make implementing it much easier.

To Do: How to Use Salesforce.com

Step 1.   Sign up.

Go to www.Salesforce.com and sign up for the version that best fits your current business. They have a variety of different options for all different budgets and businesses.

Step 2.   Make a list.

Make a list of all the different in-house activities that you want to use and track in Salesforce.com—for example, your leads, contracts, employees, emails, and pipeline. This becomes your wish list. Keep things prioritized, and star the items that are critical. Put the starred items at the top of the list so that you will work your way down your priorities at the next step.

Step 3.   Customize.

Using this list, you can see all the customizations you will need to make in order for the solution to fit your company.

Keep in mind that you can even start using Salesforce.com right out of the box. If you're a smaller company, I recommend you start using Salesforce.com as is before doing a lot of massive upgrades.

Step 4.   Specialize.

If you require a lot of additional customization, hire a certified Salesforce.com specialist. Various people know Salesforce.com well. You want someone who is a not only good programmer, but also understands processes and business flow so that he can ensure your solution suits your current needs and anticipates what additional changes you may have as you grow.

Step 5.   Train.

Train your users on how to use the system.

Step 6.   Adopt.

For any CRM solution to be effective, you must have 100 percent adoption.

Step 7. Add apps.

As your business continues to expand, consider adding different apps to your solution. Visit Salesforce.com to see all the apps it has available. Install an app or two at a time, train your users on how to use the new app, and make sure that it fits your business.

Some of my favorite apps include the following:

- **Google Integration:** This allows for documents to be linked in Salesforce.com along with outbound and inbound emails.

- **Pardot:** This is a tool for email marketing. It allows you to send highly customized emails that are also tracked in Salesforce.com. When looking at your contacts, you can segment out who viewed, deleted, opened, and clicked on the email.

- **Genius:** This app tracks open rates of emails to see how many people are reading them. With Genius, you have a little box up on your computer screen. The box tells you if anyone is viewing your email live.

- **Hoover's:** This gives us the competitive intelligence we're looking for. Hoover's provides information about the size of the company, key decision makers, recent news, and beyond. I like to be armed with as much information as possible before talking to a prospect.

Tas Tip

Here is an example of how I use Salesforce.com:

- Every lead, referral, and prospect is entered and tracked here.

- After we determine that a lead has revenue potential, we convert it into an opportunity. We forecast based on opportunities: expected close date, expected close percentage, and the dollar value.

- All customers and data are housed in Salesforce.com. Every email and greeting card sent, every phone call placed, and other activities are entered here. Anything that relates to our customers is tracked.

- All employees are tracked in Salesforce.com, including contracts, pictures, personal information, wages, job description, and the like.

- Our live events are managed with the event plug-in designed by Salesforce.com.

Tracking Your Web Site

You cannot measure, what you cannot track. It is critical to keep a close eye on the amount of traffic your web site is getting, where that traffic is coming from and how (if at all), users are interacting with your site. While there are hundreds of tracking tools, you only need a few to give you a 360-degree view on everything that is taking place.

To Do: How to Use Google Analytics (Google. com/analytics):

I've been a Google analytics user since its inception. This tool provides very robust information about who has visited your site, where they came from, what pages they visited, how long they stayed and beyond. There are lots of ways to further customize it to fit your particular business. Since this tool is so powerful, I wanted to give you a step-by-step guide on how to use it:

Step 1. Install.

Install the tracking code on your site. Make sure that the code is installed on every page on your site.

Step 2. Wait.

Wait a solid seven days before starting to look at trends. It takes some time for the data to start pulling.

Step 3. Implement.

Use the various tools to analyze and understand the data:

- **Unique Visitors:** This is the number of people who visit your site, excluding duplicates. For instance, if someone visits your site 100 times in the same day, it will not be counted more than once.

- **Page Views:** Page views represent the number of total pages viewed across your site. For instance, say you have ten visitors and 100 page views. This would mean that, among those ten people, 100 pages across your site were viewed, with an average of ten page views per visitor.

- **Bounce Rate:** This is the percentage of people who visit only one page, or exit on the page they came into. We typically consider the bounce rate as people who are not interested in what we have to offer because they didn't explore other pages the site offers.

- **Average Time on Site:** Care to know how long the average person stays on your site? This will give you that data!

- **New vs. Returning:** Seeing how many people are new to your site for the first time gives you some great information. I use this to make sure that I'm attracting new people, as well as returning visitors to my blog to read the content.

- **Traffic Sources:** This is, in my opinion, the most critical area to analyze. Traffic sources show you all the places you're getting Web traffic from. This will confirm whether the marketing tactics you're using are actually driving traffic. For example, if you spent five hours on Ustream.TV, did that actually produce some traffic?

Step 4. Enhance your understanding of who your visitors are and what they want.

More advanced tools will give you even deeper understanding of the people who are coming to your site:

- **Site Overlay:** This tool will show you the different places where people are clicking or taking action on your site. This data has caused us to do multiple redesigns to many sites. You can quickly see whether people are clicking on your opt-in, for example, or a different part of your site. If they are not taking the actions you are hoping they take, see where they are clicking and move your site around to accommodate.

- **Map Overlay:** This will show you all the different countries people are from who are visiting your site.

- **Content:** It's very powerful to see what pages attract visitors and where they typically exit. With this knowledge, you will see whether you need to beef up the content to keep your visitors longer—or entice them to return.

- **IP Banning:** To get an ever better estimate of your traffic, you can tell Google Analytics which computers to not include in your statistics (typically yours and your Web team's).

- **Goals:** Put in your conversion goals and track your progress of the number of people who purchase.

- **Event Tracking:** Track all the different traffic for a particular time-sensitive promotion.

- **Custom Reporting:** Design a report that makes the most sense for your business—for example, unique visitors week over week.

- **Browser Capability:** This will show which browsers, operating systems, and screen sizes are being used to view your site. If you know your site doesn't work well with Macs, yet 20 percent of your visitors are Mac users, you have some adjustments to make!

Step 5. Make changes.

Make changes to your web site and your marketing in relation to the data. You will quickly be able to see which marketing strategy is working.

Case Study

BuildDirect sells products in over 100 countries. Although the company used analytics on their site, it really didn't know how to grasp the true power. Company marketers started to do some more advanced things with Google analytics and adwords (such as split testing and conversion data). Once they got into a rhythm, things really started to move!

Results:

With insights from Google analytics, the company was able to grow sales by 50 percent, increase its search conversion by 37 percent, double its email marketing results, and realize a 100-percent growth in sample orders.

Following are two more tools to track your web site:

- **LuckyOrange.com:** This is one of those "hidden gems" that I often don't speak about because I don't want my competition using it. This tool allows you to record entire visitor sessions (in video), create heat maps, and much more. What I love about the visitor recording feature is the ability to watch an exact video of what my prospects did. It tracks their mouse movements, when they were idle, where they came from and beyond. The heat map feature allows you to quickly see where things are getting the most clicks so you can be certain your web sites are designed correctly.

- **Optimizely.com:** A/B split testing is critical anytime you have a web site. Web sites can always be improved to perform better, and the only way you can be sure you are making the right changes is by using a tool like this. It will quickly show you which page outperformed the other.

Search Engine Optimization

If you are not on page one of Google, your web site really doesn't exist. Not only do you need to make sure your web site is designed correctly for the search engines, you need to monitor your rankings and links in real time to make certain you are moving in the right direction. While there are hundreds of free tools out there, I've had the best luck with paid tools.

Tools include:

- **Moz.com:** Among the oldest companies in the SEO space, Moz.com delivers. Their tools will allow you to analyze things, see where your site needs to get improved, and then keep track of things to see what is working / what is not working.

- **Wordtracker.com:** I use this tool almost every single day to find the most profitable keywords that I should be targeting. While I really like the Google Keyword Tool, I find that it can be a bit biased and the numbers can be off. Wordtracker helps me level the playing field and zero in on what matters.

- **RavenTools.com:** I love to see reports, and Raventools. com delivers some beautiful reports. I often like to use this in tandem with Moz.com to compare the two reports and see if there are any discrepancies that I should look into.

Social Media Marketing

Everyone is doing some type of social media marketing and with the large number of platforms out there, keeping track of everything, automating things, and generating revenue from social media can get to be a bit of a daunting task. Like SEO, there are hundreds and hundreds of social media tools out there, but only a few have made my final cut.

Tools include:

- **Hootsuite.com:** This is extremely easy to use and allows you to manage multiple profiles in real time, schedule posts in advance, and keep a close eye on your brand. It is used by over nine people, so it must be solid!

- **Sproutsocial.com:** Although I like Hootsuite.com for my social media management, when I use to have a lot of different web sites to look after, this tool was amazing. I consider Sproutsocial.com to be a better option if you are looking for a "social CRM tool." In other words, if you want to be able to better manipulate your reports and add more contact level details, this is your tool.

- **Buffer.com:** Often while out and about, you get random ideas for content posting. Buffer allows you to add these and have them get posted at random to your various social networks.

Reputation Monitoring

Your reputation is everything in both personal and business. With the easy access to review sites and the Web in general, it is paramount that you track what is being said about you and your business online, in real time. It doesn't matter if what is being said is positive or negative, you should be replying and reacting to everything as fast as possible.

Tools include:

- **Netvibes.com:** I'm a huge fan of building a full blown listening station and this is my secret weapon in doing so. I use this to not only manage my reputation, but keep close tabs on my competition. This tool is in my top three favorite Web marketing tools.

- **Brandseye.com:** This promises accurate insights on all the social conversations taking place on the Web. I have used this in combination with Netvibes.com for great results.

Creating Landing Pages

One of the struggles in the marketing world is working with IT to get things done. I'm a huge fan of easy-to-use and easy-to-deploy tools that allow me to quickly get things done, get them in motion and start to generate results. Landing pages are a great way to test various campaigns, while keeping things laser focused on one particular agenda per landing page.

- **LeadPages.net:** This is another one of those secret weapons. This tool is largely being used by people in the Internet marketing space (always a good sign). You can create landing pages in minutes with this tool and integrate them across various different platforms.

- **Unbounce.com:** This tool is called the landing page creator for marketers. It is full featured, easy to use, and easy to deploy. I love using this tool for split testing as well.

Email Marketing

While many marketers are claiming email marketing is dead, the others are still reaping big rewards using email marketing the right way. There are only a few companies that I trust my email marketing with, and rest assured I have used pretty much every solution there is.

- **Aweber.com:** I'm one of Aweber.com's biggest fan. Its solution is easy to get up and running and manage as you start to gain more email subscribers.
- **MailChimp.com:** This is another solid tool in the email marketing space. It has a bit more flexibility from a design standpoint as compared to Aweber.com.
- **Infusionsoft.com:** Some people like to use Infusionsoft. com just for their email marketing and automation. It is robust, but not easy to use if you have a limited technical background.

Video Hosting

I hope you realize that you need to integrate video into your marketing. No longer will plain text or images alone help to increase your conversions. Rather than loading your videos onto YouTube.com and grabbing the embed code, I recommend you use a service to host the videos (thus, cutting out any ads that may show on your videos) and one that will allow your videos to load at lightning fast speeds.

Tools include:

- **Wistia.com:** I cannot say enough good things about Wistia.com. It has changed the way I do video marketing. You can load up your videos on its platform, get a code to embed the video right on your web site, and get advanced analytics about how people interact with your videos.

- **Amazon S3:** This is a cloud server that allows you to leverage the power of Amazon's extensive servers. You do need some technical background to get the system set up correctly, but once you are set up, you can roll out whatever videos you need.

Miscellaneous Tools

Following are a handful of other tools I recommend you take a look at to help you round out your digital marketing toolkit:

- **Godaddy.com:** There are many places you can buy domains, but I only trust Godaddy.com. If you have a lot of domains, check out the domain discount club for optimum pricing.

- **Rackspace.com:** Wherever you have your web site hosted at, you need to make sure it is 100% secure and 110% lightning fast. Rackspace.com is one of the top hosting companies on the planet.

- **PRweb.com:** Whenever I need to distribute press releases throughout the Web, I turn to PRweb.com. I've been using this service for years and have always achieved solid results in submitting my releases.

There you have it! The list of the tools that I use on a day-to-day basis to manage, track, and grow my various businesses. Rather than text out hundreds of different tools to find the best ones, use this list to help shortcut the process. A full listing of these tools can be found on marketinginthemomentbook.com.

Shopping Cart

If you are looking to sell something online you need to install a shopping cart on your site. This allows your prospects to place orders directly on your web site and move forward in the process, whether that means to ship a physical good or to start the process if you are a service-based business.

Tools for doing this include the following:

- **Infusionsoft.com:** I've mentioned this tool a few times already as it has difference uses. Having an all-in-one solution can help you keep things organized and stream-lined and more often than not, save money. Check out its robust shopping cart.

- **1shoppingcart.com:** This is another all-in-one tool, allowing for email, affiliate marketing, and the actual shopping cart piece.

- **Woocommerce.com:** If you use WordPress, you can enjoy the benefits of the Woocommerce WordPress plug-in. There is quite a bit of configuring you are able to do to make the shopping cart match the brand of the site as well as additional features.

If you are trying to become a very large e-commerce business, you will want to look at more robust tools such as Magento.com, Volusions.com, Bigcommerce.com, or Shopify.com.

9

Web Applications: How to Grow Your Business by Producing an App

Over the past two years, the development of different apps has been growing at an extraordinary rate. Rather than only talking about the traditional apps in your marketing, we're going to focus on getting an app produced to use as a lead generator. This app can be sold or given away for free. As you will soon learn, I am a fan of giving our applications away at no cost.

What Are Web Apps?

An *app* (which is shorthand for application) is a piece of software that may be found on your computer, on your mobile phone, or across the Web. Originally, all software programs were called apps. But recently, apps have come to be used specifically to refer to the small programs found on iPhones, Androids, and now other smartphones. They typically help you do something and make your life a little easier in a big way or distract your time in the form of a game. For example, the iPhone has an application that allows you to put your phone up to the radio (or any type of speaker) to have the app search for and find the name and musician for the song that is playing!

Using Mobile Apps in Your Digital Marketing

Before I dive in and focus on getting apps produced for your business, you should consider using apps in your digital marketing for better results. Because your phone is always with you, you might as well become more productive and take advantage of the device. There are many times when I'm speaking at a conference and use my phone to run my various businesses. Having a handful of apps on my mobile device helps the process tremendously.

Here are a few things they can help you accomplish:

- Increase the relationship building among your prospects/clients.
- Aid in the experience your prospects/clients receive.
- Make communication easier and faster.
- Help with the fun factor in your marketing.

Apps can be used pretty much anywhere. So far in this book, I've talked about:

- Microblogging
- Social networking in general
- Mobile marketing
- Virtual reality worlds
- Live streaming video

Live Streaming Video Apps

One of my favorite things to do with my mobile device is to live stream. All of the various live streaming services have apps that allow you do this. Although I focus my marketing efforts on UStream.tv, I really do like the Google hangout app and have been seeing it rise in terms of popularity.

Here is my short list of some of the apps I use on a regular basis to improve my marketing and boost my productivity:

- **Google Drive:** I run all my documents in Google and this tool makes managing everything seamless.

- **Evernote:** This is where I store every thought, web site, and clip. I also use it for audio recordings when I'm in the car.

- **Trello:** Staying organized and on task is critical, and this is the app that makes it happen.

- **Gotomeeting:** If you ever need to set up a meeting on the go, this is your tool.

- **Hootsuite:** My best ideas tend to come when I am "out and about" and I like to be in the moment with my social media marketing. Hootsuite has always been a great tool at streamlining my social media.

- **Vine:** This is your tool for publishing short videos as a social networking site.

- **Instagram:** This is your tool for social marketing purposes with photos.

- **Foursquare:** Arguably, this is the best local marketing application.

- **WordPress:** Every web site I have recently published is on the WordPress platform. This app allows me to manage my various sites remotely.

- **Analytics:** I love to see my statistics and analytics on the fly to see how the various campaigns I have taking place are doing.

There are apps I use on a regular basis, of course, but those are the main ones I recommend you check out to get things started. From a productivity standpoint, it normally is always easier and faster to do things from a physical computer, but if you are on the go and want to capture things "in the moment," leverage your mobile device that is already connected to you at the hip!

Creating Your Own Mobile App

A few years ago, having an app seemed like a luxury; only the biggest brands that had large pocketbooks could afford to have their own apps created. Now, with more developers available, the price of apps has come way down. Services have also emerged that allow you to build basic applications for a mere $20 a month and be up and running in hours versus what once took months.

Before you dive into the world of app production, I urge you to think about your end game. What is the purpose of having an application designed? You can use the apps as lead generators, profit centers, customer service tools, or even gifts for your prospects or customers. It makes sense to have several brainstorming sessions with your team to come up with some viable options.

The secret sauce to producing an app that "has legs" so to speak is to craft something that your users will have a hard time living without. My favorite examples are things that help save them time, make them money, or improve their lives. For example, the flashlight app, the marketing calendar app, the tip calculator app, and the inspiration quotes app—if your users start to integrate these apps into their daily lives, you have won, and big time.

Lead Generation and Profit Apps

The main reason people typically develop apps is to make money from selling them, or they use them as lead generators.

Here are some other ideas of applications you can develop for internal or external uses:

- Expense tracking
- General productivity
- Party planning
- Event management
- Games (people love to be entertained)
- Email management
- Music
- Shopping
- Video (streaming or static)
- Mobile

The way I approach application development is as follows:

1. We have a 50-minute strategy session in which we just throw out ideas. (No idea is bad.)
2. We think of apps we would use (or want to play with).
3. We check to see whether there is anything similar.
4. If we find nothing extremely similar, we build out the app.

And that's it. That is our process for deciding which applications to roll with. As noted with the price being so low to get apps produced, we are okay with testing the waters on a few different things to see which one sticks the

best. My mantra has always been "sloppy success." What
I mean by this is simple: I would rather put out a product
that isn't amazing while investing limited money in order to
get feedback, versus go overboard and potentially produce
something that no one will want to use. Some success
is better than no success. I've used this methodology in
everything that I've done. Having speed in your marketing is
critical.

To Do: How to Create Your Own Apps

To create your own apps, follow these steps:

Step 1. Think about it.

Figure out what you want the app to do, in terms of
functionality. Then develop a mind map or a scope.
This will save you a lot of money in the long run. If
you engage someone to get this produced and have a
blank check, your investment will skyrocket.

Step 2. Decide whether you want to give away the app or sell
it. This allows you to figure out if you should have a fair
amount of advertising in the app, or keep it relatively
clean.

Step 3. Hire a solid developer to build out the app, or use one
of the many services to launch an app quickly.

This is where things will take a turn depending on the
route that you take.

If you are looking for someone basic that is not going
to require a lot of coding, I highly recommend using
one of the services that follow to get something up
and running quickly. This typically is the best option
if you are just getting started and would like to get
something live fast. The other thing to keep in mind is
that you do not need any coding skills to get this up
and running, most of them are simply drop and drag.

Here are a variety of sites where you can get your app
launched quickly and easily:

- www.Como.com
- www.MobileRodie.com
- www.TheAppBuilder.com
- www.AppyPie.com

On the flip side of things, if you are looking to have something totally new and innovative created, you are going to need to engage a developer to help move your vision into action.

Check out www.Elance.com, www.Guru.com, www.Odesk.com, www.RentACoder.com, and www.craigslist.org for a variety of additional developers.

My word of caution is to re-read Step 1. You must have a clear, defined outcome, launch dates, milestone dates, and beyond so the process (and investment) doesn't go through the roof. I have seen this happen almost every single time. You get in the heat of the moment and start to add more features, and add more features, pushing the investment and the time frame up exponentially.

Step 4. Set up the lead-capture page to sell or give away the application.

This step applies more to the giveaway of a free application. If you're going to give something away, you have the right to ask for something in return. In this case, ask for the following information:

- Name
- Email address
- Mobile-phone number (remember, you want mobile, not general phone)
- Web site (if applicable)

Step 5. Price accordingly (if you're selling).

Keep in mind that a lower-priced product is also a great way to get people familiar with your business.

After you get them to say yes the first time, it's much easier the next time!

Step 6. Drive traffic to your page.

Remember, this is not an if-you-build-it-they-will-come age anymore. Leverage the tactics you are learning in this book to drive traffic to your application. If you are driving a lot of traffic to the page but you're still seeing minimal results, take another look at the application that was developed. Is it useful to your target market? Does it have a viral factor to it? Don't just develop applications to give away for the sake of developing applications. If they have solid value to them, you're going to get some downloads and usability.

Step 7. Create more applications as you see fit.

What's the best way to figure out which applications to develop next? Do a survey! Use a tool such as www.SurveyMonkey.com to survey your audience to see what they would like to see next.

Step 8. Modify the app for continued improvement. I pushed you to try the sloppy success mentality, getting something out there sooner than later. This method works in the long haul only if you continue to improve your app in the future to make it even better, and clean up some of the "sloppiness." Don't go crazy, but continue to improve it to make it a better experience for your end users.

Using Apps to Aid in Your Customer Experience

As you are now well aware that your prospects and customers are heavy on mobile, it makes sense to integrate apps into your customer service. Although this is not a book about providing amazing customer service, every study I have seen in the last few years has shown that the better the customer experience and service that is provided, the more users will frequent your business and tell their friends. Why not grow the experience and make it more pleasurable?

Take a look at some of the pain points in your business, the different things you have had complaints about. For example, customers may tire of checkout lines that are too long, not being able to find a salesperson to help, confusion about what to purchase, or worries about not getting the best price.

Armed with your list of pain points, take a stab at which ones you can solve. If you want to reduce the checkout times, allow people to scan their purchases in advance and go to a faster checkout line. If your store is always mobbed, have a few stations with an iPad or desktop computer that enables people to find things quickly. I rarely purchase books at a physical store anymore, but I found myself at Barnes and Noble the other day for a particular book for my kids (*Oh the Places You Will Go*, customized version). Because the book is quite popular, they of course did not have it in stock. However, within 10 feet of the section was a computer that enabled me to easily order the book from the Barnes and Noble site. Rather than walk out upset (with a lost sale on the store's behalf), I walked away only slightly upset that I didn't have the book now, and the sale was still made. Find ways to make the experience better: that is the secret formula. Have Instagram stops set up for people to take photos, stations where people can compare prices and get better reviews, charging stations for their phones, and anything that can help the experience.

Apps on Other Platforms

Everything I just mentioned focuses on "mobile apps." These are apps that are developed for use on a mobile device. The term app also applies to applications across the Web or on other devices (such as an iPad), for example. Although my intention is not to confuse you, I do want to make you aware of some other opportunities to leverage apps in your digital marketing efforts.

Some other locations you can leverage apps are:

- **On web sites:** These apps are cloud based and would be used via a desktop computer. An example of an app that I created for use on desktop computers is a strategic planning app. Because there a lot of text is being entered, it tends to perform better on a computer versus a mobile device.

- **On social media sites (for example, Facebook):** Most of the big social media sites have apps or add-ons, and chances are that these apps were created by a developer. What I like about Facebook apps is the capability for the apps to send push notifications to your friends list. Although many people get annoyed by this quickly, there are some interesting uses from a marketing standpoint. If you are invested in social media and it is proving to be a solid source of profit for your business, you may want to explore producing an app for the Facebook platform.

- **On other devices (for example, the iPad):** Some people lump the iPad into the mobile app space, but I don't because of its much larger size. My favorite use of iPad apps is in a business that has a physical footprint. A while back, my old marketing and design agency coded an app for one of the largest financial advisory firms in the United States. The app allowed prospects to play a game and find out how they think about money. What I love about the concept is it makes the scary concept of money and talking about money simple. Some other examples of iPad apps include express checkout at a store, the ability to browse what things are in stock or out of stock, an interactive restaurant menu with photos and videos so you can be sure you are making the right choice, and a contest with an opt-in form at a trade-show booth. Tablets are perfect tools to demonstrate your products and services in a fun and interactive manner, keyword interactive.

If you haven't been able to figure it out by now, I love mobile and everything about it. I encourage you to focus on mobile to start with, before exploring other avenues and other platforms. Mobile is the hottest trend, and it is here to stay. When I wrote the first edition of this book, having a mobile app was more of a luxury. With this edition, it is becoming more of a necessity. Your customers will actually start to get angry if you don't have any ways to integrate your business into their mobile device. They expect it. Dominate the entire mobile trend, and you will dominate your industry.

10

Open-Source Code: How to Find and Use Others' Hard Work for Maximum Impact

Open-source code is a big part of the digital revolution because it fits one of the key driving factors: collaboration. This chapter introduces you to open-source code.

What Is Open-Source Code?

Open-source code is developed by several people (even thousands) working together to make a usable tool or program. Even when it's finished, some of these same people (or others) can and will continue to improve on it for the goodness of all. Using open-source code can help you develop programs, tools, and even Web sites that can be used in your marketing efforts.

Behind every software program you use (for example, Microsoft Office), there is code that tells it how to function and behave. For proprietary reasons, this code is typically patented, copyrighted, trademarked, and locked up tight so that unauthorized people can't mess around with it. Developers, and the businesses for which those developers are working, don't want someone ripping off their code or taking the code and then making a similar program.

Many programmers and businesses have decided that it is in the common good to write code and then make it available to the public to improve on. I love the analogy of comparing open-source code to a potluck picnic. Everyone gets to bring something and, from the various individual contributions, a full meal is made. The concept is essentially the same. With open-source code, the meat is typically provided by another programmer, and then others are invited to add to it and make it a full, working program that people would want to use. The best part: It's free. As with a potluck, because you brought something with you, there is no cost to you.

With collaboration being the model of choice for many people, open-source code has thrown the software model on its head. The code that's behind the software tool you are running would be visible and free for use. This would be like Microsoft saying, "Hey, we know you love Microsoft Outlook, so here's the code; use the program and code for free. In fact, feel free to improve on it, make it better, and, while you're at it, sell your new software for a profit."

Using Open-Source Code

Open-source code is gaining so much popularity for many reasons:

- Everything is going to the cloud. When was the last time you actually got a physical CD for a software tool you purchased? Need to upgrade your Apple operating system? You can do it electronically in minutes. The cloud just makes sense.

- Using open-source code can save you money. Why reinvent the wheel when you can start off with something first?

- Open-source code offers the benefit of a wide diversity of collaborators who are working independently, often throughout the world, unburdened by corporate politics. The spirit of volunteerism and independent creativity fosters maverick innovation that can often lead to a stronger, more useful product.

- Collaboration is the new model. As you will learn in the next chapter, collaboration is critical for success. You cannot live in a box thinking you know everything!

There are, however, a few key disadvantages to open-source code:

- It can be costly to maintain the platform for others to collaborate on. Someone needs to maintain the server, the bandwidth, and the technology that others are collaborating on. Because open-source code is typically given away, you can spend money and go through a lot of trouble without directly benefiting from the results.

- Quality control is nonexistent. Although it is great to have many people contributing their coding and creativity, their skill levels may not be up to the quality you might expect from the big-name companies.

- As with cooking, everyone has their own style of coding. This, in my opinion, is the biggest downfall to open-source code. One person's coding style can be drastically different from the way another codes. You end up getting a final product that may have all different types of code when it could have been a bit simpler.

- You get minimal support, if any.

To Do: How to Leverage Open-Source Code

In this case, I'm talking only about how to use others' code for your business or personal use, rather than from a programming standpoint of collaborating on the code while it's in development.

Step 1. Find what you're looking for.

What type of software are you looking for? Chances are that whatever you are looking for has some type of open-source code software out there. Go to www.Google.com and type in Open Source and then whatever software you're looking for—for example, open source content-management system.

Step 1.5. See whether there is some raw code instead of an out-of-the-box solution.

Here are some sites to get the code from:

- www.code.ohloh.net
- www.SourceForge.net
- www.CodeBeach.com
- www.Planet-Source-Code.com

Step 2. Evaluate the open-source programs out there before selecting one.

As with physical software, there are typically many alternatives that accomplish the same thing. Do your research, and read the message boards, forums, and so on to choose the best software to manipulate.

Step 3. Get it going.

Start using the software as is or hire a programmer to manipulate the code. Typically you are going to want to hire a programmer to help with the coding aspect to make the software even better and to suit your needs. Also bear in mind that many open-source programs can be used with no manipulation.

Here are some of my current favorite open-source software tools:

- **Firefox:** The browser of choice for most.

- **OpenOffice.org:** Don't want to give Microsoft any more money? Leverage OpenOffice.org and their suite of tools.

- **Joomla:** Among the best content-management systems available today.

- **Drupal:** This is another content-management system. Many programmers use Drupal to configure their entire web sites and shopping carts.

- **WordPress:** This is the blogging platform of choice. I have worked on thousands of WordPress web site projects. I also use a software tool called WishList Member to design WordPress member sites. There are hundreds of people all over the world constantly working on and making WordPress better and better.

- **PortableApps:** Plain and simple, this tool aims to make all your apps portable on a USB drive. You can carry all your favorite programs on a small device and use them on any computer!

- **MediaWiki:** Originally developed by Wikipedia, it allows for easy collaboration.

Step 4. Make available the code adjustments you hired the programmer to make.

Because the open-source movement is all about collaboration, why not give back? Post the coding adjustments (as long as they are not proprietary) to the open-source community so that others can build on the changes you had made.

Tas Tip

If you drastically improve an open-source-code software tool and pay a programmer considerable money to do so, you will want to look at rebranding and selling it. Before doing so, learn about the rules and regulations of the open-source code you are using. This is a great way to make some extra money and pay for your development costs!

That's it. Using open-source code is actually quite easy. With the growing number of people looking to use open-source code rather than purchasing traditional software, chances are you will find some type of open-source software tool already out there in cyberspace to leverage and/or improve on your needs!

11

Collaboration and Speed: The Secret Sauce to Marketing in the Moment

In order to market in the moment, you must be able to respond and act quickly. We are living in a "me-centric" environment, and an environment where your customers want everything immediately. For example, close to 50 percent of people who complain on social media expect a response from you within 60 minutes or less and more than half of those people expect the same on evenings and weekends.

I'm a serial entrepreneur at heart, as noted in the introduction of this book, and I love starting and growing companies. My two "secret sauces" to every company I've started (or clients I've helped) are to dominate with marketing and nail the systems. Marketing and systems will keep you in business for the long haul.

This chapter focuses on collaboration. The better you are able to collaborate in real time, the faster you can respond in the moment to your prospects and customers.

There are hundreds of ways teams can collaborate, but I've zeroed in on the most important, the ones that will make the biggest difference to your speed and competitive edge:

- Chatting
- Sharing docs, files, audios, and videos
- Project management
- Teleconferences/webinars

Keep in mind that the software tools I recommend have been or are being used by my companies or our clients. I never recommend something I cannot deem as useful, affordable, and a tool you will see a solid ROI from. Because there are more than 15 tools I recommend, I'm not going to give you a traditional how-to, step-by-step, as I have previously. Instead, I provide some specifics you should be aware of.

Google Apps

Google Apps is a collection of tools designed and hosted by Google. Google Apps started off with Google Mail and has expanded drastically from there. For $50 a year (at this writing), you get the following:

- Email accounts
- Calendars
- Google Drive (docs, spreadsheets, forms, and presentations)
- Chatting capabilities (voice and text)
- Mini portal sites
- Contact management
- And much more (check out

To Do: How to Implement Google Apps in Your Company

To implement Google Apps in your company, follow these steps:

Step 1. Sign up.

Go to www.google.com/a and sign up for Google Apps.

Step 2. Verify.

Follow the technical details on how to verify your domain name. Typically, it simply means posting a page on your site to prove you have ownership.

Step 3. Configure.

Configure your email. This will involve changing your MX records wherever your Web site is hosted. This tells your hosting company that Google is now hosting your email. Your email will be example@yourdomain.com.

Step 4. Create.

Create your different user accounts for all your employees and "virtual employees." Keep in mind that there is a small fee, so don't get crazy, but also don't skimp!

Step 5. Personalize.

Set up your email settings, under the Settings tab, when logged in to Google Apps.

- Set up a signature.
- Link it with Microsoft Outlook or other mail clients, if applicable.
- Set up filters. Instead of using traditional folders, Google Mail uses something called filters. This allows you to direct any mail that comes from janedoe@janedoe.com to a filter called Jane Doe.
- Color-code things to your liking for easier access.

Step 6. Schedule.

After you have your email set up, move to your calendar. If you're a Microsoft Exchange user, this will save you money. Have your employees use their Google calendars and share accordingly. Depending on your structure, some people should be able to help manage your calendar, with others having only viewing privileges. This, too, can sync with your mobile phone and Microsoft Outlook.

Step 7. Centralize.

Get everyone to use Google Docs. I love the mail and calendar apps, but I adore Google Docs! Here, you can create, edit, and manage the following:

- Documents (such as Microsoft Word documents).
- Spreadsheets (such a Microsoft Excel documents).
- Presentations (such as Microsoft PowerPoint documents).
- Forms (any type of paper document that you need someone to fill out can be designed in here and submitted virtually).

What is awesome about Google Docs is that multiple people can view a document, form, spreadsheet, or presentation at the same time and make changes with each other live. This solves the issue of some people not having the most up-to-date version of a particular document.

These are some uses (there are thousands):

- Collaborating on your marketing calendar
- Pulling in analytical reports
- Sharing company documents, such as your handbook and policies
- Keeping track of usernames and passwords with spreadsheets

- Managing personal or business finances
- Keeping résumés in one place
- Requesting vacation time off, using a Google form

Make sure that, after creating the file, you click on the Share Files link. Invite people who will view the document and those who should be able to make changes to it.

Step 8.   Link.

Set up mini portal sites. You can set up unlimited mini portal sites and share them with the appropriate persons. We have used these for managing different projects. These portal sites then allow you to link to the various other Google Apps.

Step 9.   Leverage.

Leverage some of the many other Google Apps:

- **Mobile:** Get your apps right on your phone.
- **Google short URLs (like www.tinyurl.com):** Make the URL much easier to remember.
- **Google web sites:** Publish simple web sites with ease.
- **Contacts:** A great contact-management system to keep your contacts information stored and updated virtually.

Step 10.   Follow up.

Collaboration is only as good as the collaborators using the tools available to them. So make sure your team is using their collaboration tools to their fullest extent. You can't have some people sending docs through email, others through Google Docs, some on Google's mail system, and others on something else. Your goal is 100 percent adoption.

Case Study

I am constantly launching new web sites and web site re-design projects. As you are well aware, there are many moving parts to a web site launch. Because we are Google Apps fanatics, we launched a mini portal site devoted to the redesign of our web site. We invited the seven people who were involved in the design process.

On the portal site, we had the following:

- A calendar that everyone could see and manage with all the critical dates, meetings, and deadlines.
- Google forms to be filled out daily, reporting on progress.
- A spreadsheet with the links to the different pages that would be on the site.
- A presentation on the vision of the site that everyone could come back and watch to make sure that the build out was in line with the blueprint.
- Fifty-plus Google documents with all the new web site content, shared with our copywriters.
- A countdown tool showing how many days we had left until the launch date.

It was wonderful to have one central place to have all of this information to collaborate.

The takeaways are:

- This tool saved us time and money from having to conduct dozens of unnecessary phone calls and long email exchanges.
- Everything was virtual, so we could access it from anywhere.
- We launched the site three weeks ahead of schedule.

Tas Tip

Without full user adoption implementing new systems will not be of service to you. Understand that in the beginning, adoption may take some time to get everyone fully utilizing the new tools and systems, but in the long run, everyone has got to be on the same page.

Collaboration Tools

Following are a handful of tools that allow you to collaborate in real time from essentially anywhere on the planet. All you need is an internet connection.

Collaboration Tool 1: Chatting

You need to be able to communicate with your team quickly and effectively. With the costs of travel rising, chatting with video has become more popular. Rather than purchasing expensive hardware, leverage one of the many free or low-cost tools. Most new computers already have built-in functionality to make chatting much easier than before.

Picking one tool and using it exclusively is a much better strategy than using various chatting platforms. I also recommend using video whenever possible. Because I have a large virtual company and rarely see people face to face more than once a year, it's nice to see their smiling faces on webcam from time to time!

Tools to use include the following:

- **Google Hangouts:** Because I recommend you become a Google-driven company, it makes sense to leverage Google's chatting tools. You can use both gchat and Google Hangouts for quick collaborating.

- **www.Skype.com:** We replaced our VOIP-phone systems with Skype for a huge savings. All of our employees, contractors, and vendors are required to use Skype to chat with us. We use text chat for quick questions, voice for conference calls and meetings, and video when conducting one-on-one meetings. We also have started using one of Skype's newest features, screen sharing, making it an even greater all-in-one solution. This allows you to view someone else's desktop in real time.

- **www.ooVoo.com:** This application allows you to chat over the Web with text, voice, and video. The advantage of ooVoo is that you can see multiple people's webcams as opposed to only one.

Collaboration Tool 2: Sharing Docs, Audios, Videos, and Files

Because the chances of you and everyone else being on the same network are slim to none, you need to have a central place and Web systems in place to share and work on together with ease.

Digital storage and file sharing is critical. You need to keep backups on hard drives, as well as in digital locations. With file sharing, it's great to be able to work with your team on documents at the same time and see who has accessed and downloaded certain files.

Tools to use include the following:

- **Google Apps:** You can share and work on documents, spreadsheets, and presentations all in one place.

- **www.Box.net:** I use this tool for two things. First, I have an account where I back up my hard drive daily. Second, we have a company account. If clients want to send us large files (like audio or video), we ask them to upload the files to Box.net and then share them with us. There is a free version of Box.net as well as a paid one allowing you more storage and faster uploads.

Collaboration Tool 3: Project Management

There are a lot of moving pieces to marketing. Tracking all the different pieces can be a nightmare because there are typically different people working on different parts at different times. More important, there are always different things that need to be finished before you can move onto something else. This is like the game Jenga. If you pull out pieces here and there, the whole tower can come crashing down. Much as with chatting collaboration, you can't leverage multiple project-management tools. It doesn't make sense to have different pieces in different locations.

Tools to use include the following:

- **Google Apps and Sites:** The earlier case study details how we used Google Sites to manage the launch of our new and improved web site. It's very easy to use. The only drawback is the inability to set clear tasks with follow-up actions.

- **www.AtTask.com:** Similar in nature to Basecamp, AtTask enables you to manage multiple projects, tasks, and workflow modules. The tool is relatively straightforward and is also being used by a lot of top companies.

- **www.teamwork.com:** I use to be a big user of Basecamp until I found Teamwork.com. I have turned Teamwork.com into my central hub for all things project management and collaboration. I have seen case studies of companies running almost their entire operation using this tool. I highly recommend you check it out.

Collaboration Tool 4: Teleconferences and Webinars

We use teleconferences and webinars to collaborate with each other, our prospects, and our clients. In terms of effectiveness when trying to close business, we prefer to use a webinar because it allows us to give visuals, making things easier to understand. When we're delivering presentations to the masses, we tend to just use audio and conduct these in the evening, when most people will have finished eating. We use audio for these larger groups because a lot of people will be multitasking or listening on a mobile phone while driving. If we need to make a key point using visuals, those people are going to miss the boat completely.

Tools to use include the following:

- **www.GoToWebinar.com:** GoToWebinar allows you to have a phone bridge of up to 1,000 people and share your screen or presentation. We use this tool when we're conducting educational presentations to both prospects and our virtual team.

- **Adobe Connect:** This tool has a clean-cut platform that's easy to use. Adobe Connect is starting to pick up some steam in the Web conferencing arena.

- **www.WebEx.com:** This tool is Cisco's product. It competes directly with GoToMeeting and GoToWebinar.

- **www.FreeConferencecallhd.com:** A 1,000-line phone bridge for free! I'm sure this will change, but it will be low cost. I use this tool almost daily.

Start collaborating "in the cloud" with your team and you will be able to outpace your competition every single time. The more things you bring into the cloud, the better. This allows your entire company to get aligned and have access to the same information in real time, thus being able to capitalize on marketing potential in real time. Get in the cloud and never look back!

12

Digital Marketing Superstars

This chapter provides seven different companies for you to take a look at. One model I have used for years is called *modeling*. If I know someone else is succeeding in a big way, I look at figuring out how they are doing it and replicate the process. Why would I start from scratch when someone else has already paved the way? The intention of giving you a list of some companies is to help spark some innovation. Check out these companies to hopefully light a spark under you.

Company: Fro Knows Photo

Web site: www.froknowsphoto.com

I love stories of people turning their passions into full-time businesses. Fro Knows Photo is a site that is dedicated to all things photography. The site has lots of amazing content. I actually used the content to set up my digital SLR camera and was walked step by step through the process.

What I love about Fro Knows Photo from a digital marketing standpoint:

- The author's videos are totally different than most stuff out there. The name of the site came from his ever-so-large afro that is apparent in all the videos. He also stays true to his brand and starts all his videos with "Fro Knows Photo." Repetition in marketing—I like it.

- The author's blog is updated often, and it's full of videos, infographics, pictures, and more.

- He loves to interact with his followers. There is a place where you can submit photos for consideration on his web site.

- His podcast has been updated over 100 times and is one of the most listened to podcasts on Itunes.com.

- He has more social media followers than some Fortune 1000 companies! At the time of writing this chapter, more than 114,000 people follow him on Facebook, for example, and there are 44 million views on his YouTube videos.

Company: Kegworks.com

Web site: www.Kegworks.com

Kegworks.com sells tools for drinking. The company sells everything from draft beer equipment and bar supplies, to premium cocktail ingredients and other unique drinking accessories. Kegworks not only has an amazing e-commerce site, but it also has a physical storefront.

What I love about its digital marketing is:

- It dominates with search engine optimization. I checked about 15 different keywords and they were on page one, often #1 for all of them. Google watermelon tap, for example; it dominates page one.

- It boasts over 28,000 fans on Facebook. Yes, big numbers, but what really impresses me is the authentic helpfulness they use in their social media. Questions are answered in real time (or close to it) and with thoughtful responses.

- There are several educational videos (and some fun ones) on Youtube.com. The bottle cap wall video has over 100,000 views.

- The blog is updated daily with a lot of great content. The key is consistently posting on a regular schedule.

- The company is also on Instagram, Google+, and Pinterest.

Company: Lyods Taco Truck

Web site: www.whereslloyd.com

There has been a birth of a new industry in Buffalo, New York; food trucks. Lyods Taco Truck is known around Buffalo as one of the best places to get a taco. The company serves great food from morning until night, and it has taken the city by storm. What I love about its digital marketing:

- There is a reliance almost entirely on social media to drive business.

- Twitter and Facebook pages are updated in real time and sometimes dozens of times a day.

- They stay up to date on all of their local listings and are monitoring their reputation, commenting on all the various reviews they receive.

- My favorite thing: They are transparent and authentic.

Company: Plastic Printers

Web site: www.Plasticprinters.com

When you think of printing on plastic, you think of plastic printers. The company prints business cards, loyalty cards, gift cards, VIP cards, access cards, credit cards, and more. In looking at its client list (among the most impressive client list I have ever seen), you can tell it's a company that means business and is best in class.

Here are a few things Plastic Printers does extremely well from a digital marketing perspective. This list is derived from firsthand experience, as just a few weeks ago, I used them to print my business cards (I switched from metal to plastic):

- The company rocks when it comes to live chat. Replies are instant and employees work insanely long hours, ensuring they don't miss a beat. You can tell fun is part of the company as the message is, "Save me from Angry Birds monotony, and please let me help you."

- From a search engine standpoint, it dominates the competition. This is largely due to the size of the site, the amount of content, and the number of solid backlinks.

- The email marketing and follow-up process is second to none. The company over communicates, does surveys, and asks for testimonials.

- The site is full of helpful content including articles, blog posts, and lots of great videos.

Company: River Pool Spas

Web site: www.riverpoolspas.com

River Pool Spas is a pool installer in and around Virginia. I have been following the company for quite some time when I heard the owner of the company speak about his strategy to blogging (which blew me away). Having just gotten an in-ground pool installed in my backyard, I was able to go through the experience and landed on the simple fact that pool companies need to do a 360 with their marketing if they want to survive. River Pool Spas dominates the market-place!

What I love about its digital marketing:

- It provides more educational content on its blog than any company I have ever seen. This is the key to strategy and also its secret sauce for how to survive the recession.

- Google pretty much any phrase related to pools and it comes up #1, not simply on page one, but the #1 spot.

- By removing the secrecy to the process and being upfront and transparent, the company rules the space. It actually provides content that its competitors completely shy away from: for example, pricing or pros and cons to the various types of pools.

- The focus is almost entirely on blog marketing. Although this strategy makes me a bit nervous, I would much rather see you knock one digital marketing area out of the park versus doing four or five different tactics at an average rate.

Company: The Points Guy

Web site: www.thepointsguy.com

There is big business in credit cards. The "points" guy quit his job and started a full-time business that is his passion—racking up credit card miles and points in order to do fun things. The business model is simple: He earns money every time someone follows through on credit card offerings that he recommends. The content is great and it's a site that I enjoy reading (which is hard to come by).

What I love about its digital marketing follows:

- Similar to River Pool Spas, the blog is updated daily, if not multiple times a day. At the time of writing, he has posted over 20 times in three days.

- The content is meaty content. There is limited fluff. In many cases, I feel he goes a bit overboard, but I prefer to see content that is more meaty than less.

- He personally replies to almost every question and comment. Many people start blogs and start posting, but ignore the comments.

- The engagement factor is high. There are different specials, giveaways, and prizes during the week.

- His social media presence is great. He is on all the major platforms and is posting like a machine.

Company: TD Bank

Web site: www.tdbank.com

While all the other examples I just provided were "not huge" companies, I wanted to end this chapter with a company that is a bit larger: TD Bank. It has branches all over the place. Normally, banking content is quite bland, but TD Bank does things quite differently. As I'm writing this chapter, TD Bank just came out with, in my opinion, one of the greatest videos I have ever seen.

What I love about its digital marketing:

- They don't act or post like "bankers;" their content is different from most. Yes, they jump on comments and reply to things in real time related to banking, but their content strategy as a whole is quite different from most other banks.

- Its viral video has already been viewed by over 8 million people; by the time of printing, I wouldn't be surprised if it's closer to 100 million people. Make sure you check out the video on Youtube.com.

- TD Bank accomplishes the wow factor with its video and has surprised its customers with something truly amazing.

- An integrated a hash tag in the video, #TDthanksyou, is getting thousands of thousands of tweets and responses of which they have been replying to.

13

Your Action Plan: Putting It All Together and Taking Action

Now you're armed with all the tools to kick your marketing and business strategies up a notch. The final step is, of course, putting it all together.

What I've noticed after attending and speaking at hundreds of conferences throughout the world is that people get very excited about the material, but a month or two later will be at the exact same place as they were when they heard the new material. Don't let that happen to you. This is the art of analysis paralysis. I totally get it; I've been there many times. Focus on action and the right actions that this book taught you.

SWOT Analysis

To set a clear action plan and some goals, you need to know where you currently are (remember the 360-degree review you did in the beginning?), as well as where your competitors are. To do this, I'm going to use the ever-popular SWOT analysis. A SWOT analysis is a strategic approach to looking at the Strengths, Weaknesses, Opportunities, and Threats of a project, a business, or something of that nature. It is meant to help you quickly see things in a logical chart so you can plan accordingly. To make things easier to understand, I'm going to use a company I once owned as a case study.

To Do: How to Conduct a SWOT Analysis

Follow these steps to conduct a SWOT analysis:

Step 1. Grab a piece of paper and fold it in half.

Fold it in half again so you have four squares. You can also do this virtually, if you would like.

Step 2. Label the four squares Strengths, Weaknesses, Opportunities, and Threats.

Step 3. List your thoughts and ideas about your marketing in the different columns.

Make sure you don't leave anything out.

- **Strengths:** Where are things excelling? What are you good at? What's going well?

- **Weaknesses:** Where are things not going so well? What needs work?

- **Opportunities:** In what areas do you see potential growth? What areas should be explored?

- **Threats:** Where are the obstacles you may run into? What are the possible issues and areas to watch out for?

Here are some marketing-specific questions to ask yourself to better complete this activity:

- What digital marketing tactics are you using/not using?

- What sites are you on/not on?

- Do you track everything?

- What type of analytical information are you getting back?

- How is the presentation of your materials?
- What feedback did you get from your customer surveys?
- What is the marketplace asking of you?
- How is your web site?
- What type of interaction takes place in your marketing?
- How are you generating leads?

This list can go on forever. The idea is to ask the tough questions and then get real with the responses. You want a good mix of strengths, weaknesses, opportunities, and threats.

Step 4. Relax.

After making a first pass at the strengths, weaknesses, opportunities, and threats, take a day and let the ideas sit.

Step 5. Try again.

Give the SWOT analysis one more pass and add any new items you might have come up with during that day of rest.

Step 6. Research the competition.

After you have your SWOT analysis complete, move on to your competitors. Research your top three to five competitors and perform the same SWOT analysis on them.

Obviously, you won't have insider information to know all their analytics and hard data, but there are plenty of free tools out there that will give you some good insight. www.Alexa.com is good for gathering basic analytical statistics for any site. It just takes a bit of investigating and some patience to find things on the Web.

Ask the same questions you asked before, but now about the competition. For example:

- How does their web site look?
- What digital marketing tactics are they using?
- What are their customers or prospects saying?
- What data can be retrieved from sites like www. Alexa.com?

Step 7. Get an objective perspective.

Now that you have a SWOT analysis on your company, as well as a few competitors, have an outside party do a SWOT analysis on both your company and your competitors. Your analysis may be slightly skewed if you rely solely on your own judgment, either too critical or not critical enough. Locate your local SCORE chapter and take your information to them or post the project on a site like www.Guru.com or www.Elance. com for paid freelance help. Do not, however, show them your work. Their information needs to be fresh without any influence.

Step 8. Set goals.

Using this information, create your SMART goals for the next three to six months.

Case Study

Guerrilla Video Solutions is a video production and editing company that specializes in web videos, corporate videos, training videos, and commercials, essentially all things video shooting and editing. Although most of their business is local, they wanted to expand out into national video editing and production.

Guerrilla Video Solutions SWOT Analysis of Web Presence

Strengths:

- Videos doing well on Youtube.com, getting lots of comments and views.

- Good reviews and feedback on the product.
- SEO is off to a great start.
- Local listings are secured and ranking well.

Weaknesses:

- Social media presence is lacking engagement and larger numbers.
- Traffic is low in general from outside the local area.
- Bounce rate is on the higher side.

Opportunities:

- Use more frequent blog posts.
- Mobile play—start grabbing mobile numbers.
- Additional products can be added.
- Capitalize on the live video trend.

Threats:

- Major competition both locally and nationally.
- More and more companies popping up from freelancers and people outside the U.S.
- Many competing companies have much larger marketing budgets or still don't see video as the best place to put their marketing dollars.

Using this information, they revised their marketing plan, added several new product offerings, and have started to generate non-local sales for the first time in the history of the company!

Your Action Plan for the Next Three to Six Months and Beyond

It's great to talk strategy and formulate ideas, but it's another thing to implement them. Don't get into analysis paralysis with these marketing ideas; formulate a clear plan of action.

I like to identify SMART goals and then follow up with three to five action items under each. I have been using SMART goals for years, and it works best for me because there is little to be interpreted or misunderstood.

To Do: How to Set SMART Goals with Follow-Up Actions

To set SMART goals with follow-up actions, follow these steps:

Step 1.   Make your SMART goals.

To get you started, set no more than five SMART goals, because each goal is going to be followed up with action steps.

Example of a good SMART goal: Close $10,000 in new business by December 31.

Example of a poor SMART goal: Generate some new revenue soon.

Again, remember that SMART goals are specific, measurable, attainable, realistic, and timely. Only you will know if the goal is attainable, and the other attributes are easy to identify. Always have a timestamp on your SMART goals. How can you plan without any specific dates?

Step 2.   Make a list.

Take each SMART goal and list three to five specific action steps that need to be accomplished to move you closer to that goal. What you will notice is that the action steps under each main SMART goal are also SMART goals themselves, in a way. It doesn't help if your SMART goals are great but your action steps aren't clear.

Here are some SMART goal examples:

SMART goal #1: Design a new web site for under $10,000 by January 15.

- Interview five design firms by October and hire the one that fits the job best.

- Make a copy of the current web site for backup purposes.
- Assign one staff member to a project-manager role to aid the design firm.

SMART goal #2: Launch a fully designed blog by September 15.

- Hire a WordPress expert to design the blog.
- Load content to the blog by September 1.
- Test the blog on different browsers and operating systems to ensure compatibility by September 10.

SMART goal #3: Perform SWOT analysis on the current market by September 30.

- Develop and send a customer survey using www.SurveyMonkey.com by September 1.
- Analyze the customer-survey feedback by September 10.
- Perform the SWOT analysis.
- Hopefully see where new markets are present from the previous data.

Step 3. Revise and adjust your SMART goals, as needed.

If the timelines or numbers need to change, do so as needed, but make sure you keep things in line with the SMART-goal formula.

Step 4. Complete the action steps to make sure you hit the goals.

Tas Tip

This is where 95 percent of people falter. They set the SMART goals but don't take any action steps to reach these goals. The minute you write down the action steps, make sure you initiate: Put things on your calendar, start soliciting résumés or bids for the different jobs, take action, and you will be ahead of 95 percent of entrepreneurs looking to reach the top! The old saying "90 percent of life is just showing up" needs a huge adjustment. Let's revise it to "90 percent of life is not just showing up, but taking clear and consistent action steps after you get there."

The Areas You Should Start with Immediately

I've discussed a lot of digital marketing ideas in this book. It's up to you to pick and choose which ones can be easily adapted to fit your business. To help you, I wanted to identify the four areas you should focus on first. You have only so many hours in the day. Spend those hours on the three things covered next.

Mobile

This trend cannot be ignored (unless you don't mind getting passed by your competition). Make sure your web site is mobile responsive. Tackle that project first. Once you have that completed, start to capture mobile phone numbers and get them into a mobile marketing campaign. I urge you to keep mobile at the forefront of all of your marketing efforts. If you are exhibiting at a trade show or event, know that that your prospects will have their mobile device; cater to that as a simple example. If I were to look a few more years out, I see a day where everything is done on a mobile device (and I mean everything).

Video

I cannot stress video enough. Two years ago, it was fine to have a video camera and post some things from time to time. Today, consumers expect video sales pages, video testimonials, and video walk-ons (where you appear on your site with a welcome message). The companies that do not have video are being seen as inferior and outdated, and it is, quite frankly, costing them sales.

If you have not used video before, start small. Get yourself a camera, and upload a few informational videos on www.YouTube.com. Don't be surprised or upset if they don't get 14 million views. Just get into the habit of shooting videos and posting them online.

After you get a bit more comfortable with the camera, post a video to your blog and solicit feedback. Chances are, you're going to get some great feedback and praise for the information. This will kick you up a notch to full-blown video shooting. Start shifting everything to video: testimonials, blogs, and descriptions. Give your audience lots to watch!

After you have done this (or if you're already an advanced videographer), conduct a video audit. Ask these questions:

- Do you have videos on?
- All your sales pages on?
- Your site product descriptions?
- Your home page?
- Weekly (or daily) video blogs?
- YouTube?

Next, take your video up a notch by adding some walk-in or walk-out music. Either learn to do this editing yourself or hire a video expert. You can really jazz up videos!

Only after you have mastered static videos should you move on to live! Host a trial event on Ustream.TV and then a real one. If you get a bit more daring, keep a regular schedule for these live video events to acquire a consistent following.

Collaboration Tools

Not only will the tools I presented help your marketing, but they will help your business in general. Go back through the chapter on collaboration and see what tools you can immediately start using. I'm confident that there are least a few you haven't adopted yet.

Get yourself on Google's platform—and you won't look back! After you have this down, make sure your customer relationship management system is helping your business rather than hurting it. If you don't have a CRM system, get one. (Again, I recommend www.Salesforce.com.)

Tas Tip
Virtual collaboration is the way business is being done today!

If you maintain an office with in-house staff, consider letting them work from home. My entire company is 100% virtual with contractors throughout the world. This one tip has helped save our clients millions of dollars every year. This is the way the world is moving.

Social Networking

Although this this is not a new trend, many of the platforms are brand new or changing on a regular basis. Focus on the platforms that you can make an authentic and regular contribution on. Focus on providing content that people say "wow that was great." This is the way content gets spread and the way you get more eyeballs on your business.

The network of choice (where you should focus on dominating first) should depend on the type of business you operate. If you have a visual product, I would focus quite heavily on Pinterest. If you are in the B2B market, then LinkedIn should be at the top. You get the picture.

Keep an eye out for new networks that are niche specific. Dominate by providing more content compared to your competitors.

Final Thoughts on the Evolution of the Web

The Web is changing constantly. Never stop reading and continuing your education. Stay on top of the current trends so that your business can constantly be ahead of that curve, leaving your competitors in the dust.

In the first edition of the book, I gave you a list of trends I saw evolving. I do the same thing here; surprisingly, many of these trends are still on the list (I guess I was a few years ahead of my time):

- **Mobile:** The smartphone device will evolve to rival a computer. You will pay for everything with your device, hosting all your medical information and running your entire life (and potentially business) with that device.

- **Video:** Most of the shooting you will do will be from a tablet or smartphone. No longer will hiring video studios be a necessity to produce high-quality materials.

- **Ads:** Traditional ads will be replaced with native ads. Billboards will be out of business. The entire ad market will do a 360. Email marketing will start to get replaced with social media ads and SMS messages.

- **Blogging:** Blogging will stay strong as one of the best places to put content and attract organic traffic. No longer, though, will short blog posts be the norm. Full-blown e-books, infographics, and whitepapers will be expected.

- **Searching:** Google, like always, will continue to evolve its platform. There will be several more search changes that destroy rankings for many companies, with the true authentic ones still standing. Social media and search will go hand in hand. It will become near impossible to rank your site without a large social media presence.

- **Social networking:** Hundreds of thousands of smaller, more private social-networking sites will pop up, and many will be made by ordinary people with open-source technology.

- **Virtual reality worlds:** People will start getting over the fact that they think it's weird and start adopting it. This will be fueled by Facebook's recent entry into the virtual reality world space.

- **Wearable technology:** You will start to wear more and more technology type devices. Your shirt will serve as a charging station for example. These wearable devices will start to play a huge role in the marketing and advertising space.

- **Workplace:** The general workplace structure will continue to get more informal and collaborative. Businesses will start allowing more employees to work from home and take advantage of the various web-based collaboration tools. Flextime will become the norm, along with smaller teams.

Conclusion: The Art of Taking Action

One of the favorite times in my life was the startup days of the digital agency I use to own. Not only was the startup vibe a lot of fun, but at the time, the bulk of my clients were speakers, authors, coaches, and consultants. I actually got some of my first clients from the amazing web site Craigslist. As I was able to make my first author widely successful, he referred me to someone else, who referred me to someone else, and things just started growing like weeds. Long before I knew it, 100 percent of my clients fit in the speaker / author genre.

You might be thinking, "Where is he going with this?" Because of all of these speaker type clients, I got to go to hundreds of events in a short time span. My request to my client was simple: Let me blend in with the crowd and get to know and network with the attendees.

What I found at these events was quite shocking. Before I tell you what I found, please note that I am not bashing anyone in the speaking industry. Heck, I am a speaker myself. I simply want to shed light on one massive problem that is most likely standing in your way to more digital marketing success.

At these events, the bulk of the people I talked to were "in awe" of the speaker / presenter. They loved the feeling they got from being at these events, the atmosphere, the networking, the special events, and yes, even the food. I call this the "conference high." You experience a high from being immersed in an amazing event. I've experienced this many times.

After people gave me details about why they were there, how many events they had attended, and a few other random details, my final, direct question to them was simple: What actions have you taken as a direct result of the event? Nine times out of ten, I would get a blank stare or a different tone that would turn a bit rude, as I had people I talked to on "blast." I wasn't trying to be rude; I was trying to help people correlate attending and learning to action and more success. Most of the attendees would rather continue to attend events than take action.

I love learning, I love attending live events and buying training programs, but I am addicted to taking specific targeted actions that will increase my cash in the bank. Actions lead more success in your digital marketing. I gave you the roadmaps and the step-by-step processes to implement everything. Take action and your bank account will grow.

I am not a fan of the word someday. It is one of my least favorite words in the English language. Don't leave this book saying that someday you will get rolling with mobile marketing or someday you will tackle social media. Someday never comes. The time is now!

It has been an honor getting to share this material with you. I always love hearing from my readers and can be contacted via email at michael@nojokemarketing.com.

To your continued and future health, wealth, and happiness,

Michael S. Tasner Jr.

Index